The Delia Collection
Fish

BBC
BOOKS

Published by BBC Books
BBC Worldwide Ltd
Woodlands
80 Wood Lane
London W12 OTT

First published in 2003
Reprinted 2003, 2007

A proportion of these recipes has been
published previously in *Delia Smith's Winter
Collection*, *Delia Smith's Summer Collection*,
Delia's How To Cook Books One, *Two* and *Three*,
*Delia Smith's Complete Illustrated Cookery
Course*, *Delia Smith's Christmas*, *Delia's Red Nose
Collection* and *Delia's Vegetarian Collection*.

Edited for BBC Worldwide Ltd
by New Crane Ltd

Editor: Sarah Randell
Designer: Paul Webster
Sub-editor: Heather Cupit
Picture Editor: Diana Hughes
Recipe Testing: Pauline Curran
Commissioning Editor for the BBC: Vivien Bowler

ISBN 978 0 563 48733 3

Printed and bound in Italy
by L.E.G.O SpA
Colour separation by Radstock Reproductions Ltd
Midsomer Norton

Cover and title page photographs: Michael Paul
For further photographic credits, see page 136

Introduction

When I look back over my years of cookery writing, I have to admit that very often, decisions about what to do have sprung from what my own particular needs are. As a very busy person who has to work, run a home and cook, I felt it was extremely useful to have, for instance, summer recipes in one book – likewise winter and Christmas, giving easy access to those specific seasons.

This, my latest venture, has come about for similar reasons. Thirty three years of recipe writing have produced literally thousands of recipes. So I now feel what would be really helpful is to create a kind of ordered library (so I don't have to rack my brains and wonder which book this or that recipe is in!). Thus, if I want to make a fish recipe, I don't have to look through the fish sections of various books, but have the whole lot in one convenient collection.

In compiling these collections, I have chosen what I think are the best and most popular recipes and, at the same time, have added some that are completely new. It is my hope that those who have not previously tried my recipes will now have smaller collections to sample, and that those dedicated followers will appreciate an ordered library to provide easy access and a reminder of what has gone before and may have been forgotten.

Delia Smith

Conversion Tables

All these are approximate conversions, which have either been rounded up or down. In a few recipes it has been necessary to modify them very slightly. Never mix metric and imperial measures in one recipe, stick to one system or the other.

All spoon measurements used throughout this book are level unless specified otherwise.

All butter is salted unless specified otherwise.

All recipes have been double-tested, using a standard convection oven. If you are using a fan oven, adjust the cooking temperature according to the manufacturer's handbook.

Weights

½ oz	10 g
¾	20
1	25
1½	40
2	50
2½	60
3	75
4	110
4½	125
5	150
6	175
7	200
8	225
9	250
10	275
12	350
1 lb	450
1 lb 8 oz	700
2	900
3	1.35 kg

Volume

2 fl oz	55 ml
3	75
5 (¼ pint)	150
10 (½ pint)	275
1 pint	570
1¼	725
1¾	1 litre
2	1.2
2½	1.5
4	2.25

Dimensions

⅛ inch	3 mm
¼	5
½	1 cm
¾	2
1	2.5
1¼	3
1½	4
1¾	4.5
2	5
2½	6
3	7.5
3½	9
4	10
5	13
5¼	13.5
6	15
6½	16
7	18
7½	19
8	20
9	23
9½	24
10	25.5
11	28
12	30

Oven temperatures

Gas mark 1	275°F	140°C
2	300	150
3	325	170
4	350	180
5	375	190
6	400	200
7	425	220
8	450	230
9	475	240

Contents

White Fish

Fried Plaice Fillets
with a Herb and Polenta Crust
Serves 2

2 plaice fillets (about 6 oz/
175 g each), skinned

1 teaspoon finely chopped
fresh rosemary or 1 dessertspoon
finely snipped chives

1 teaspoon finely chopped
fresh thyme

2 oz (50 g) polenta

2 cloves garlic, very finely chopped

finely grated zest and juice of
2 small lemons

1 large egg

2 tablespoons olive oil

salt and freshly milled
black pepper

A good way to avoid making breadcrumbs, and therefore save time, is to keep a packet of polenta (cornmeal) in the cupboard. It makes an excellent coating for all types of fish, and here we've used it, along with garlic, herbs and lemon, to coat plaice fillets. You can use lemon or Dover sole instead of plaice if you prefer.

This couldn't be simpler. Just combine the herbs, garlic and polenta on a flat plate. Then add the lemon zest, along with a good seasoning of salt and pepper. Mix it all evenly, then wipe the plaice fillets with kitchen paper.

Beat the egg in a shallow dish, dip the fillets in the egg and coat them with the polenta mixture, pressing it on well.

Now take a very large frying pan and heat the oil in it over a high heat. When it is good and hot, add the fish, then turn the heat down to medium and cook the fish for about 2-3 minutes on each side, depending on the thickness. Drain on absorbent kitchen paper and serve on hot plates with the lemon juice squeezed over.

Fillets of Sole Véronique
Serves 2 as main course or 4 as a starter

2 good-sized Dover or lemon sole, (about 12 oz-1 lb/350-450 g each), skinned and filleted

3 oz (75 g) grapes, Muscat type, if you can get them

½ oz (10 g) butter, plus a little extra for greasing

1 heaped teaspoon chopped fresh tarragon

6 fl oz (175 ml) vermouth or dry white wine

½ oz (10 g) plain flour

5 fl oz (150 ml) whipping cream

salt and freshly milled black pepper

You will also need an ovenproof serving dish.

This famous French classic has always been a favourite of mine and I love to serve it with the grapes well chilled, which beautifully complements the warm, rich sauce. However, if you prefer, you could add the grapes to the fish before it goes under the grill.

First, peel the grapes well in advance by placing them in a bowl and pouring boiling water over them. Leave them for 45 seconds, then drain off the water and you will find the skins will slip off easily. Cut the grapes in half, remove the seeds, then return them to the bowl and cover and chill in the fridge until needed.

When you are ready to start cooking the fish, begin by warming the serving dish and have a sheet of foil ready. Then wipe each sole fillet and divide each one in half lengthways by cutting along the natural line, so you now have 8 fillets. Season them and roll each one up as tightly as possible, keeping the skinned side on the inside and starting the roll at the narrow end. Next, put a faint smear of butter on the base of a medium frying pan and arrange the sole fillets in it. Then sprinkle in the tarragon, followed by the vermouth or dry white wine. Now place the pan on a medium heat and bring it up to simmering point. Cover, then put a timer on and poach the fillets for 3-4 minutes, depending on their thickness. While the fish is poaching, pre-heat the grill to its highest setting.

Meanwhile, take a small saucepan, melt the butter in it, stir in the flour to make a smooth paste and let it cook gently, stirring all the time, until it has become a pale straw colour. When the fish is cooked, transfer the fillets with a fish slice to the warmed dish, cover with foil and keep warm. Reserve the poaching liquid. Next, boil the fish-poaching liquid until it has reduced to about a third of its original volume. Stir in the cream and let that come up to a gentle simmer, then gradually add this mixture to the flour and butter paste in the small saucepan, whisking it in well until you have a thin, creamy sauce. Taste and season with salt and freshly milled black pepper. Pour the sauce over the fish and pop it under the pre-heated grill, about 4 inches (10 cm) from the source of the heat, and leave it there for 3-4 minutes, until it is glazed golden brown on top. Serve each portion on to warmed serving plates, garnished with grapes.

Fried Skate Wings
with Warm Green Salsa
Serves 2

1 lb (450 g) skate wings
(2 small or 1 large cut in half)

1 heaped tablespoon
seasoned flour

2 tablespoons groundnut or
other flavourless oil

For the green salsa

1 medium clove garlic

½ teaspoon sea salt

4 anchovy fillets, drained and
finely chopped

1 heaped tablespoon capers,
rinsed and patted dry

1 heaped teaspoon wholegrain
mustard

1 tablespoon chopped fresh basil

2 tablespoons chopped fresh
flat-leaf parsley

2 tablespoons fruity olive oil

juice of 2 large limes
(4 tablespoons)

freshly milled black pepper

Skate wings have everything going for them. They have a fine-flavoured, creamy flesh that comes away from the bone with no fuss or bother, and they're dead easy to cook. I love them shallow-fried to a crisp, golden colour, with the following sharp and quite gutsy salsa poured in at the last moment. Serve with a mixture of dressed green salad leaves and some tiny new potatoes. The salsa also works well with fried cod steaks or any other fried white fish.

I think it's preferable to make the salsa not too far ahead as the parsley tends to discolour, though you could make up most of the salsa in advance and add the parsley at the last moment – either way, it's very quick and easy. All you do is crush the clove of garlic with the ½ teaspoon of sea salt, using a pestle and mortar (or on a board using the back of a tablespoon) till you get a paste-like consistency. Then simply combine this with all the other salsa ingredients and mix everything very thoroughly.

To cook the skate wings, take a large frying pan (10 inches/25.5 cm) and put it over a gentle heat to warm up while you wipe the skate with kitchen paper and coat them with a light dusting of the seasoned flour. Now turn the heat up to high, add the oil to the pan and, as soon as it's really hot, add the skate wings. Reduce the heat to medium and fry them for 4-5 minutes on each side, depending on their size and thickness. To test if they are cooked, slide the tip of a sharp knife in and push to see if the flesh parts from the bone easily and looks creamy white. Then pour in the salsa all round the fish to heat very briefly. It doesn't need to cook but simply to warm a little. Serve the fish straightaway with the salsa spooned over.

Thai Fish Curry with Mango

Serves 4 generously

2 lb (900 g) firm fish fillet
(such as Greenland halibut, cod
or haddock), skinned and chopped
into 1½ inch (4 cm) chunks

1 large mango, peeled and cut into
¾ inch (2 cm) pieces

2 x 400 ml tins of coconut milk

For the curry paste

2 medium red chillies, halved
and deseeded

grated zest and juice of 1 lime

2 stems of lemon grass,
roughly chopped

1 inch (2.5 cm) piece of fresh root
ginger, peeled and sliced

4 cloves garlic, peeled

1 small onion, peeled
and quartered

1 teaspoon shrimp paste

3 tablespoons Thai fish sauce

To serve

3 tablespoons chopped fresh
coriander leaves

You won't believe how utterly simple and easy this recipe is, and yet it tastes exotic and wonderful and, what's more, it can all be prepared well in advance and the fish added about 10 minutes before you want to eat it.

Begin by emptying the coconut milk into a large, deep frying pan or wok and stir while you bring it up to the boil, then reduce the heat to medium and cook until the fat separates from the solids. What will happen is the coconut milk will start to separate, the oil will begin to seep out and it will reduce. Ignore the curdled look – this is normal. You may also like to note that, when it begins to separate, you can actually hear it give off a crackling noise. This will take 20 minutes or so, and you will have about 1 pint (570 ml) left. Now make the curry paste, and all you do is put everything in a food processor or blender and whiz until you have a rather coarse, rough-looking paste and everything is perfectly blended.

Then, over a medium heat, add the curry paste and fish to the pan and, once it has reached simmering point, give it 4 minutes. Finally, add the mango and cook for a further 2 minutes. Serve the curry with the coriander sprinkled over and Thai fragrant rice as an accompaniment.

Note You can prepare the curry in advance. Make everything up, keeping the paste covered in the fridge, then, 10 minutes before you want to serve, bring the coconut milk back up to the boil and add the paste, fish and mango, as above.

Roasted Monkfish with Romesco Sauce
Serves 6

2 lb (900 g) monkfish tail
(weight when boned and skinned)

4 tablespoons extra virgin olive oil

a squeeze of lemon juice

salt and freshly milled
black pepper

For the sauce

3 large cloves garlic, peeled

3 fresh ripe plum tomatoes

1½ oz (40 g) hazelnuts

1 large egg yolk

2 small dried chillies

8 fl oz (225 ml) extra virgin olive oil

2 tablespoons sherry vinegar

To garnish

a few sprigs of flat-leaf parsley

lemon wedges

Pre-heat the oven to gas mark 4,
350°F (180°C).

This recipe was given to me by Clare Hunter, a very talented person who used to cook for private dinner parties on an old Thames sailing barge. The pungent, nutty romesco sauce makes a perfect partner to monkfish and this would be an ideal recipe for entertaining.

First, to make the sauce, put the whole garlic cloves, tomatoes and hazelnuts into a shallow roasting tray in the oven for 10 minutes, then add the chillies. Cook for another 5 minutes until the hazelnuts are golden. Scrape the flesh from the tomatoes and put into a blender with the egg yolk, chillies, hazelnuts and garlic. Blend on high speed and add the olive oil slowly to make a smooth sauce. Next, stir in the vinegar, season lightly, cover and leave aside.

Take the fish from the fridge 30 minutes before you need it, to allow it to reach room temperature. When you are ready to cook the fish, turn the oven up to gas mark 6, 400°F (200°C) and lightly oil the fish fillets. Heat a large frying pan, add the remaining oil and, when it is very hot, put the oiled fillets in and lightly brown them on all sides. Transfer them to a roasting tray and cook on the top shelf of the oven for 10-15 minutes, depending on the thickness of your fish. Remove from the oven, season with salt and freshly milled black pepper and sprinkle over some lemon juice. If necessary, reduce the juices from the fish by letting them bubble over a high heat.

Slice the fillets across the diagonal on to warmed serving plates, pour over a little of the fish juice and serve with the romesco sauce, sprigs of parsley and lemon wedges. Clare serves this with some Puy lentils cooked in red wine with thyme and dressed with olive oil and balsamic vinegar.

Luxury Fish Pie
with Rösti Caper Topping
Serves 4-6

For the fish mixture

1 lb 8 oz (700 g) halibut

8 oz (225 g) king scallops, including the coral, cut in half

4 oz (110 g) raw, peeled tiger prawns, defrosted if frozen

5 fl oz (150 ml) dry white wine

10 fl oz (275 ml) fish stock

1 bay leaf

2 oz (50 g) butter

2 oz (50 g) plain flour

2 tablespoons crème fraîche

6 cornichons, drained, rinsed and chopped

1 heaped tablespoon chopped fresh parsley

1 dessertspoon chopped fresh dill

salt and freshly milled black pepper

For the rösti caper topping

2 lb (900 g) Desirée or Romano potatoes, evenly sized if possible

1 tablespoon capers, rinsed and patted dry

2 oz (50 g) butter, melted

2 oz (50 g) strong Cheddar cheese, finely grated

You will also need a 2½ pint (1.5 litre) baking dish, about 2 inches (5 cm) deep, well buttered.

Pre-heat the oven to gas mark 7, 425°F (220°C).

This is a perfect recipe for entertaining and wouldn't need anything to go with it other than a simple green salad. The fish and shellfish can be varied according to what's available, as long as you have 2 lb 4 oz (1 kg) in total.

First of all, prepare the potatoes by scrubbing them, but leaving the skins on. As they all have to cook at the same time, if there are any larger ones, cut them in half. Then place them in a saucepan with enough boiling, salted water to barely cover them and cook them for 12 minutes after they have come back to the boil, covered with the lid. Strain off the water and cover them with a clean tea cloth to absorb the steam.

Meanwhile, heat the wine and fish stock in a medium saucepan, add the bay leaf and some seasoning, then cut the halibut in half if it's a large piece, add it to the saucepan and poach the fish gently for 5 minutes. It should be slightly undercooked.

Then remove the fish to a plate, using a draining spoon, and strain the liquid through a sieve into a bowl. Now rinse the pan you cooked the fish in, melt the butter in it, whisk in the flour and gently cook for 2 minutes. Then gradually add the strained fish stock little by little, whisking all the time. When you have a smooth sauce, turn the heat to its lowest setting and let the sauce gently cook for 5 minutes. Then, whisk in the crème fraîche, followed by the cornichons, parsley and dill. Give it all a good seasoning and remove it from the heat.

To make the rösti, peel the potatoes and, using the coarse side of a grater, grate them into long shreds into a bowl. Then add the capers and the melted butter and, using two forks, lightly toss everything together so that the potatoes get a good coating of butter. Now remove the skin from the white fish and divide it into chunks, quite large if possible, and combine the fish with the sauce. Next, if you're going to cook the fish pie more or less immediately, all you do is add the raw scallops and prawns to the fish mixture then spoon it into a well-buttered baking dish. Sprinkle the rösti on top, spreading it out as evenly as possible and not pressing it down too firmly. Finally, scatter the cheese over the surface and bake on a high shelf of the oven for 35-40 minutes.

Roasted Fish topped with Sun-dried Tomato Tapenade
Serves 6

6 cod or haddock fillets (6-7 oz/ 175-200 g each), skin removed

salt and freshly milled black pepper

For the tapenade

10 oz (275 g) jar sun-dried tomatoes, drained, reserving the oil

6 oz (175 g) pitted black olives in brine, drained and rinsed

1 oz (25 g) fresh basil leaves

2 fat cloves garlic, peeled

1 heaped teaspoon green peppercorns in brine, rinsed and drained

2 oz (50 g) anchovy fillets, including the oil

3 heaped tablespoons capers, rinsed and patted dry

3 tablespoons oil from the tomatoes (see above)

freshly milled black pepper

You will also need a large baking sheet, lightly oiled.

Pre-heat the oven to gas mark 6, 400°F (200°C).

This is, quite simply, a fantastic recipe – it takes no time at all but has the kind of taste that makes people think you spent hours in the kitchen. And another of its great virtues is that, apart from the fish itself and fresh basil leaves and garlic, the whole thing is made from storecupboard ingredients.

Begin by reserving 6 whole olives and 6 medium basil leaves from the ingredients, then all you do to make the tapenade – which can be made 2 or 3 days in advance – is place all the ingredients in a food processor and blend them together to a coarse paste. It's important not to overprocess; the ingredients should retain some of their identity.

When you're ready to cook the fish, wipe the fillets with kitchen paper, season, then fold them by tucking the thin end into the centre, then the thick end on top of that so you have a neat, slightly rounded shape. Turn them over and place on the oiled baking sheet, then divide the tapenade mixture equally among them, using it as a topping. Press it on quite firmly with your hands, then lightly roughen the surface with a fork. Dip the reserved basil leaves in a little of the reserved tomato oil and place one on top of each piece of fish, following that with a reserved olive. Now place the baking tray on a high shelf in the oven, bake the fish for 20-25 minutes, and serve straightaway.

Oriental Steamed Fish with Ginger, Soy and Sesame
Serves 4

1 lb 8 oz (700 g) lemon sole fillets, skinned and cut lengthways down the natural dividing line

2½ inch (6 cm) piece of root ginger, peeled

1 tablespoon Japanese soy sauce

1 rounded tablespoon sesame seeds

3 cloves garlic

2 spring onions

1 dessertspoon sesame oil

1 dessertspoon groundnut or other flavourless oil

juice of 1 lemon

a few outside lettuce leaves or foil for lining the steamer

salt and freshly milled black pepper

You will also need a bamboo or fan steamer.

This can be a quick supper dish for the family, or it's exotic enough for entertaining: all you need is a steamer – bamboo or the old-fashioned fan kind.

Begin this by having a little chopping session. First, the ginger, which should be thinly sliced, then cut into very fine shreds. The garlic needs to be chopped small, as do the spring onions, making sure you include the green parts as well.

Now place a medium frying pan over a medium heat and, when it's hot, add the sesame seeds and toast them in the dry pan, shaking it from time to time until they're a golden brown colour – this takes only 1-2 minutes. Now transfer the seeds to a bowl.

Next add the oils to the pan and, over a medium heat, gently fry the chopped garlic and ginger – they need to be pale gold but not too brown, so take care not to have the heat too high. After that, add these to the toasted seeds, along with any oil left in the pan, then mix in the lemon juice, soy sauce and chopped spring onions.

Now season the fish, then spread three-quarters of the mixture over the surface of each skinned side, roll them up quite firmly into little rolls, then spoon the rest of the mixture on top of each roll. All this can be prepared in advance, as long as the fish is kept covered in the fridge.

Then, when you're ready to cook the fish, line the base of the steamer with the lettuce leaves (or foil if you don't have any). Now place the fish on top, cover with a lid and steam over boiling water for 8-10 minutes. Serve with stir-fried rice.

Flaky Fish Pie
Serves 4

For the pastry

8 oz (225 g) plain flour, plus a little extra for dusting

6 oz (175 g) butter

a pinch of salt

beaten egg, to glaze

For the filling

12 oz (350 g) any white fish (such as haddock, cod or whiting)

about 15 fl oz (425 ml) milk

1 oz (25 g) butter

2 tablespoons plain flour

1 tablespoon capers, drained and chopped

4 small gherkins, drained and chopped

2 tablespoons chopped fresh parsley

2 large eggs, hard-boiled and chopped

1 tablespoon lemon juice

salt and freshly milled black pepper

You will also need a baking sheet, 11 x 14 inches (28 x 35 cm), greased.

This is a wonderful recipe that transforms the humble haddock, cod or whiting into something really special. If you're short of time, you can use ready-made puff pastry instead (you'll need a 500 g pack).

To make the pastry, first of all, remove a pack of butter from the fridge, weigh out 6 oz (175 g), then wrap it in a piece of foil and return it to the freezer or freezing compartment of the fridge for 30-45 minutes.

Then, when you are ready to make the pastry, sift the flour and salt into a large, roomy bowl. Take the butter out of the freezer, fold back the foil and hold it in the foil, which will protect it from your warm hands. Then, using the coarse side of a grater placed in the bowl over the flour, grate the butter, dipping the edge of the butter into the flour several times to make it easier to grate. What you will end up with is a large pile of grated butter sitting in the middle of the flour.

Now take a palette knife and start to distribute the gratings into the flour – don't use your hands yet, just keep trying to coat all the pieces of fat with flour. Then sprinkle 2-3 tablespoons of cold water all over, continue to use the palette knife to bring the whole thing together, and finish off, using your hands. If you need a bit more moisture, that's fine – just remember that the dough should come together in such a way that it leaves the bowl fairly clean, with no bits of loose butter or flour anywhere. Now pop it into a polythene bag and chill for 30 minutes before using.

To make the filling, place the fish in a medium saucepan with just enough milk to cover, bring to the boil, cover and simmer gently for about 5-10 minutes. Now strain off the milk into a measuring jug and, when the fish is cool enough to handle, flake it into large pieces (discarding all the bones and skin), place in a bowl and set aside. Next, melt the butter in the same saucepan and stir in the flour. Cook for about 2 minutes over a medium heat, then gradually add 10 fl oz (275 ml) of the milk the fish was cooked in, stirring all the time. Bring the sauce to the boil, simmer gently for 6 minutes, stirring from time to time, then take the pan off the heat and add the flaked fish, chopped capers, gherkins, parsley and eggs. Season with salt, pepper and lemon juice. Cover and leave until the mixture is quite cold.

When you're ready to cook the pie, pre-heat the oven to gas mark 7, 425°F (220°C). On a lightly floured surface, roll out the pastry to a 12 inch (30 cm) square, trimming, if necessary. Lift the square on to the greased baking sheet, then place the cold fish mixture in the centre. Glaze around the edge of the pastry with beaten egg, then pull the opposite corners of the pastry to the centre and pinch all the edges together firmly, so you have a square with pinched edges in the shape of a cross. Glaze all over with beaten egg and decorate with any pastry trimmings. Glaze these, too, and then bake the pie for about 30 minutes or until the pastry is well risen and golden.

Roasted Fish with a Parmesan Crust
Serves 2

1 lb (450 g) plaice fillets (4 fillets)

3 oz (75 g) freshly grated Parmesan

4 oz (110 g) white bread, slightly stale, cut into cubes

a handful of fresh parsley leaves

2 oz (50 g) melted butter, plus a little extra for brushing and drizzling

salt and freshly milled black pepper

To garnish

1 lemon, cut into quarters

a few sprigs of fresh parsley

You will also need a baking tray, 11 x 16 inches (28 x 40 cm), lined with some kitchen foil.

Pre-heat the oven to gas mark 8, 450°F (230°C).

This works superbly well with plaice, but sole would be excellent, or thicker fish fillets, such as cod or haddock, in which case allow 5 minutes' extra cooking time. I don't feel this needs a sauce, but a green salad with a lemony dressing would be a good accompaniment.

First of all, brush the foil on the baking tray generously with melted butter. Now wipe the fish with kitchen paper, then lay it on the foil and season with salt and black pepper. Next, place the cubes of bread and parsley leaves in a food processor and switch on the motor to whiz it all to fine crumbs, then add the Parmesan, melted butter, $\frac{1}{2}$ teaspoon salt and some pepper, and pulse again to mix them in.

Now spread the crumb mixture over the fish fillets, drizzle over a little more melted butter and then place the baking tray on a high shelf in the oven for 7-8 minutes, or until the crumbs have turned a golden brown. Serve with the lemon quarters to squeeze over and a sprig of parsley as a garnish.

Pepper-crusted Monkfish with Red Pepper Relish
Serves 4

2 lb (900 g) monkfish
(weight when boned and skinned)

1½ rounded tablespoons mixed
whole peppercorns

2 rounded tablespoons plain flour,
seasoned with 1 teaspoon salt

4 tablespoons olive oil

For the red pepper relish

2 medium red peppers,
deseeded and cut into strips

2 medium tomatoes, skinned and
halved, or tinned Italian tomatoes
would be fine

1 fat clove garlic, peeled

3 anchovy fillets, chopped

1 tablespoon balsamic vinegar

1 tablespoon olive oil

salt and freshly milled
black pepper

sprigs of watercress or fresh
coriander leaves, to garnish

Filleted monkfish can be quite pricey, but there is no waste with head or bones. It has a lovely, firm, meaty texture, and I think this particular recipe would be a superb choice for someone who wants to cook something quite special but has very little time. The pieces of fish are coated with crushed mixed peppercorns and this simplest of sauces not only tastes divine but looks amazingly colourful in contrast to the fish.

Begin the relish by heating the oil in a medium saucepan. When it's really hot, add the strips of pepper and toss them around, keeping them on the move so they get nicely toasted and browned at the edges. Then add the tomatoes, the whole garlic clove and the chopped anchovies. Give it all a good stir, put a lid on and, keeping the heat at its lowest possible setting, let the whole thing stew gently, stirring once or twice, for 25 minutes or until the peppers are soft. Then whiz the whole lot to a coarse purée in a blender or food processor. Taste and season with salt and freshly milled pepper, then empty into a serving bowl and stir in the balsamic vinegar. It is now ready for serving and can be made in advance.

To cook the fish, first cut it into small rounds about ¾ inch (2 cm) thick. Crush the peppercorns with a pestle and mortar – or using the end of a rolling pin in a small bowl – to a fairly course texture, then combine them with the seasoned flour.

Next, heat the oil until very hot in a good solid frying pan. Dip each piece of fish in the flour and peppercorn mixture, pressing them gently on all sides to get an even coating. Now fry the fish in two batches, for about 2-3 minutes on each side, until they're tinged nicely brown. Keep the first batch warm while you cook the second. Serve, garnished with watercress or fresh coriander sprigs, and the sauce handed round separately.

Thai Fish Cakes with Sesame and Lime Dipping Sauce

Serves 4 as a main course or 8 as a starter

1 lb (450 g) any white fish fillets, skinned and cut into chunks

1 stem lemon grass, roughly chopped

1 fat clove garlic, peeled

½ inch (1 cm) piece fresh root ginger, peeled and roughly chopped

3 tablespoons fresh coriander leaves, plus a few sprigs, to garnish

2 kaffir lime leaves, roughly chopped (if unavailable, leave them out)

zest of 1 lime (the juice goes in the sauce)

1 medium red chilli, deseeded

½ small red pepper, deseeded and roughly chopped

3 oz (75 g) coconut milk powder

2 tablespoons lightly seasoned plain flour

2-3 tablespoons groundnut or other flavourless oil for frying

salt and freshly milled black pepper

For the dipping sauce

1 teaspoon sesame seeds

1 tablespoon sesame oil

1 tablespoon lime juice

1 dessertspoon Thai fish sauce

1 tablespoon Japanese soy sauce

1 medium red chilli, deseeded and very finely chopped

The ingredients list for these noble little Thai-inspired fish cakes looks very long, but the good thing is they can be made and cooked with incredible speed. Serve them as a first or main course, or they're also good as canapés to serve with drinks, in which case make them smaller.

To make the fish cakes you first of all need to put the lemon grass, garlic, ginger, coriander leaves, kaffir lime leaves, lime zest, chilli and red pepper into a food processor, then turn the motor on and blend everything fairly finely. After that, add the chunks of fish, process again briefly until the fish is blended in, then, finally, pour in the coconut milk powder through the feeder tube. Switch on the motor again, but be careful at this stage not to overprocess – all you need to do is briefly blend it all for 2-3 seconds.

Then tip the mixture into a bowl, add some seasoning and shape the fish cakes into 24 fairly small, thin, flattish, round shapes about 2 inches (5 cm) in diameter. If you like, you can make them ahead to this stage, but spread them out in a single layer, cover with clingfilm and keep them in the fridge till needed.

Meanwhile, make the dipping sauce. To do this, first of all begin by toasting the sesame seeds. Using a small, solid frying pan, pre-heat it over a medium heat, then add the sesame seeds and toast them, moving them around in the pan to brown them evenly. As soon as they begin to splutter and pop and turn golden, they're ready – this will take 1-2 minutes. Then remove them from the frying pan to a serving bowl and simply stir in the rest of the ingredients.

When you're ready to cook the fish cakes, first coat them in the seasoned flour, then heat 2 tablespoons of the oil in a large frying pan (10 inches/25.5 cm) over a high heat and, when it's really hot, turn the heat down to medium and fry the fish cakes briefly for about 30 seconds on each side to a pale golden colour. You will need to cook them in several batches, adding a little more oil, if necessary. As they cook, transfer to a warm plate and keep warm. Serve with the dipping sauce, garnished with the reserved coriander sprigs.

Californian Grilled Fish
Serves 2

2 fish fillets (such as cod, hake, whiting, or 2 plaice or sole – anything you like – approximately 7 oz/200 g each)

2 tablespoons Coriander and Lime Tartare Sauce (see page 129)

2 tablespoons white or brown breadcrumbs

3 tablespoons grated Cheddar cheese

1 dessertspoon chopped fresh coriander

a pinch of cayenne pepper

grated zest of ½ lime

½ oz (10 g) butter

salt and freshly milled black pepper

You will also need a grill pan, lined with foil and smeared with a trace of butter.

Pre-heat the grill to its highest setting.

If you have a jar of lovely Coriander and Lime Tartare Sauce (see page 129), a wonderful way to use it is to spread it on to some fish fillets, then sprinkle with cheese and breadcrumbs and pop them under a pre-heated grill. You'll have one of the fastest and most delectable suppers imaginable.

Begin by wiping the fish fillets with kitchen paper to get them as dry as possible, then place them in the foil-lined grill pan. Season with salt and pepper, then spread the tartare sauce all over the surface of the fish.

Now, in a bowl, mix the breadcrumbs, cheese, coriander, cayenne and lime zest together, then sprinkle this over the fish as evenly as possible. Dot with a little butter. Place the grill pan as far from the heat as possible and grill the fish for 10-15 minutes, depending on its thickness – it should be just cooked through and the top should be crispy and golden. Serve with tiny new potatoes, tossed in chives and lemon juice, and a plain lettuce salad.

Steamed Cod with Nori and Soba Noodle Salad
Serves 2

10 oz (275 g) skinless cod fillet

2 sheets toasted nori seaweed

1 tablespoon Japanese soy sauce

1 tablespoon Thai fish sauce

2 tablespoons Japanese pickled ginger, to serve

For the noodle salad

7 oz (200 g) dried soba noodles

3 tablespoons Japanese soy sauce

3 tablespoons lime juice

½ teaspoon toasted sesame oil

about 6 sprigs of fresh watercress

a pinch of salt

You will also need a bamboo steamer or a fan steamer.

This is a wonderful combination of flavours and textures – and only contains half a teaspoon of oil between two people! In the photograph we used green tea soba noodles – buckwheat noodles made with green tea – but if you find these difficult to get, ordinary soba noodles are fine. Most of the other ingredients are readily available in all supermarkets.

First of all, cut the cod into 8 equal pieces measuring about 1½ x 2 inches (4 x 5 cm), then mix these with the soy sauce, fish sauce and 2 tablespoons of water in a medium bowl. Now stir the cod around, cover it with clingfilm and leave it to marinate in the fridge for about an hour, stirring it around once or twice in that time.

While the fish is marinating, make the soba noodle salad. What you do here is – as for pasta – have plenty of water boiling in a largish saucepan with a little salt added. Boil the noodles, without a lid, for exactly 3 minutes, then drain them in a colander and let the cold tap run on them while you lift and shake them with your hands. (They need to be cooled down quickly, otherwise the heat makes them sticky.) After that, shake off all the excess water and place the noodles in a bowl. Now whisk the soy sauce, lime juice and sesame oil together and pour this over the noodles, mixing well, so they are coated in the dressing.

Now for the fish. Towards the end of the marinating time, place the steamer over a pan of boiling water. (Pre-heating it will prevent the nori sticking.) When you're ready to cook the fish, cut each of the nori sheets into quarters, then take one of them and lay it, shiny side down, on a clean, flat surface. Now take a pastry brush, dip it into the fish marinade and brush the nori. Then place a piece of cod in the centre. First, fold in 2 opposite sides, then brush the 2 remaining flaps with a little more of the marinade and wrap them over the fish, too, to form a tight parcel. (Don't worry if some of the fish is not covered.) Then repeat this with the remaining 7 pieces of fish and quarters of nori. To cook them, place all the parcels, seam side down, in the steamer, put a lid on and steam them for 5 minutes. Then serve them with the noodles, garnished with the watercress, and hand the pickled ginger around separately.

Sea Bass with Puy Lentil Salsa
Serves 2

2 sea bass fillets
(7-8 oz/200-225 g each)

1 teaspoon olive oil

½ lime, cut into wedges

sea salt and freshly milled
black pepper

For the lentil salsa

1½ oz (40 g) Puy lentils
(no need to soak), rinsed

1 large tomato

¼ medium red onion

1 small red chilli,
halved and deseeded

2 tablespoons fresh
coriander leaves

juice of 1 lime

salt and freshly milled
black pepper

This is an extremely fast supper dish for two people that is full of colour and flavour. Some small new potatoes would make a good accompaniment, but for serious waist watchers, I don't think it really needs it.

Begin by making the lentil salsa. Place the lentils in a small saucepan with 4 fl oz (120 ml) water and some salt. Next, bring them up to simmering point and gently simmer, without a lid, for about 30 minutes, or until they are tender but still have some bite and retain their shape, by which time most of the water will have been absorbed.

While the lentils are cooking, skin the tomato. Do this by placing it in a heatproof bowl and pouring boiling water on to it. After exactly a minute, remove it from the water and slip off the skin (protecting your hands with a cloth if the tomato is hot), then halve it and squeeze out the seeds. Now chop it into small pieces. After that, chop the onion and chilli very small, and the tomato and coriander, and keep all this aside, covered in clingfilm, until needed.

When the lentils are cooked, empty them into a bowl and while they are still warm, toss them in the lime juice. Now taste to check the seasoning and add the rest of the prepared salsa ingredients. Mix well and leave aside in a cool place.

To cook the fish, you need to pre-heat the grill to its highest setting for at least 10 minutes. Next, line a grill tray with kitchen foil, brush the fish fillets on both sides with the oil and place them on the tray flesh side up. Season with salt and freshly milled black pepper, then grill for 5-6 minutes, turning halfway through, or until just cooked through. Serve straightaway with the salsa and some lime wedges to squeeze over.

Salmon Trout

Salmon Steaks with Avocado and Crème Fraîche Sauce
Serves 6

For the salmon

6 fresh salmon steaks
(6 oz/175 g each)

6 small sprigs of fresh tarragon
or parsley

6 small bay leaves

1 small lemon, thinly sliced

6 dessertspoons white wine

salt and freshly milled
black pepper

For the sauce

1 good-sized avocado

7 fl oz (200 ml) crème fraîche

1 small clove garlic, peeled

1 teaspoon sherry vinegar

salt and freshly milled
black pepper

To garnish

1 bunch watercress
or other pretty leaves

Pre-heat the oven to gas mark 4,
350°F (180°C).

If you want to serve something really special for a summer dinner party that leaves you utterly free from any hassle, this cold salmon dish fits the bill perfectly. Although this recipe serves six, you can in fact line up the salmon steaks in any number you like – 12 or even 24 – which makes it ideal for buffet parties and celebrations. In winter this recipe works equally well served with Parsley Sauce (see page 111).

First of all, take a large sheet of foil (24 x 36 inches/60 x 90 cm) and lay it in a shallow baking tin. Wipe the pieces of salmon with kitchen paper and place each one on the foil. Now put a small sprig of tarragon or parsley on top of each one, along with a bay leaf and a slice of lemon (these ingredients are there simply to perfume the salmon very subtly without altering its flavour). Now season with salt and pepper and finally, spoon a dessertspoon of wine over each salmon steak before wrapping the whole lot loosely in the foil. Make a pleat in the top to seal it. Place the foil parcel on a highish shelf in the oven for exactly 20 minutes. Then remove the tin from the oven and let the salmon cool inside the foil without opening it.

Meanwhile, prepare the sauce. Halve the avocado, remove the stone, then divide into quarters and peel off the skin, using a sharp knife if necessary. Place the flesh in a liquidiser or food processor then, using a teaspoon, scrape the avocado skin to remove the last greenest part and add that to the rest. Now pop in the garlic clove, then measure in the sherry vinegar, add salt and pepper and blend until smooth. Next, remove the purée to a mixing bowl and simply fold in the crème fraîche till it's thoroughly blended. Taste to check the seasoning – it might need a spot more vinegar. Cover the bowl with clingfilm and keep in the fridge until you're ready to serve. This should be made only a few hours in advance to keep the luscious green colour at its best.

When you're ready to serve the salmon, undo the foil and, using a sharp knife, ease off the strip of skin around the edge of each steak and discard it. Remove the herbs and lemon, then transfer the fish to a serving dish and decorate with small bunches of watercress or other leaves placed in the hollow centre. Hand round the sauce separately.

Chinese Steamed Trout
with Ginger and Spring Onions
Serves 2

2 rainbow trout (8 oz/225 g each),

1 inch (2.5 cm) piece of fresh root ginger, peeled and cut into thin strips

4 spring onions

1 clove garlic, sliced thinly

1 dessertspoon crushed sea salt

For the sauce

1 teaspoon peeled, grated fresh root ginger

1 clove garlic, chopped

3 tablespoons Japanese soy sauce

3 tablespoons Shaosing (Chinese brown rice wine)

1 teaspoon toasted sesame oil

½ teaspoon dark soft brown sugar

You will also need a bamboo steamer or a fan steamer.

As with salmon, trout is slightly higher in fat, but still very low compared with meat. The fat in both trout and salmon is the good kind we all need to include in our diets. If you're wondering what the pink bits are in the photograph, they're pink spring onions, which looked very pretty the day we took the picture!

First of all, rinse the trout and dry them with kitchen paper, then sprinkle the outside of the fish with salt and leave aside for half an hour to help firm up the flesh. Meanwhile, place all the sauce ingredients in a small saucepan, then bring them up to simmering point and simmer for 5 minutes.

Next, the spring onions should be cut in half where the green and white parts meet, and the very green part cut in diagonals (making diamond shapes when opened out). The rest should be thinly shredded lengthways.

When you're ready to cook the trout, wipe the salt away with some more kitchen paper and place the fish in the steamer, with the ginger and garlic scattered inside and all over. Place it over boiling water and steam with a lid on for exactly 15 minutes. Serve the trout with the re-heated sauce poured over and garnished with the spring onions. Plain basmati rice would be a good accompaniment.

Thai Salmon Filo Parcels
Serves 2

2 middle-cut fillets of salmon
(4-5 oz/110-150 g each)

4 sheets filo pastry (approximately
7 x 12 inches/18 x 30 cm each)

1 teaspoon grated fresh ginger

grated zest and juice of 1 lime

1 clove garlic, crushed

1 tablespoon chopped
fresh coriander

1 small spring onion, finely sliced

1 oz (25 g) butter

salt and freshly milled
black pepper

To serve

a few sprigs of coriander

1 lime, cut into quarters

Pre-heat the oven to gas mark 5,
375°F (190°C).

For waist-watchers and the health-conscious the growing popularity of filo pastry is, I'm sure, warmly welcomed. But I also suspect we could be in danger of overkill, so I like to use it only where it's really appropriate – like here, where a parcel of something really does seal in all those precious salmon juices, and when they mingle with the lime, ginger and coriander, the result is marvellous!

First of all, in a small bowl, mix together the ginger, lime zest, garlic, coriander and spring onion, then stir in the lime juice. Now melt the butter in a small saucepan, then lay 1 sheet of filo pastry out on a flat surface, brush it all over with some of the melted butter, spread another sheet of filo on top and brush this lightly with melted butter as well.

Now position one of the salmon fillets near to one end of the filo, season it and sprinkle half the lime and herb mixture on top. Next, fold the short end of pastry over the salmon, then fold the long sides inwards, roll the salmon over twice more and trim any surplus pastry (it's important not to end up with great wedges of pastry at each end). Wrap the other piece of salmon in exactly the same way and, when you're ready to cook, brush the parcels all over with melted butter, place them on a lightly greased baking sheet and bake in the oven for 20-25 minutes or until the pastry is brown and crisp. Serve, garnished with sprigs of coriander and wedges of lime to squeeze over.

Foil-baked Whole Fresh Salmon with Green Herb Mayonnaise
Serves 8

4 lb (1.8 kg) fresh whole salmon

2 oz (50 g) butter, plus extra for buttering the kitchen foil

1 small onion, thinly sliced

3 bay leaves

4 sprigs of fresh tarragon

salt and freshly milled black pepper

For the green herb mayonnaise

2 large eggs

2 teaspoons mustard powder

1 fat clove garlic, peeled

10 fl oz (275 ml) groundnut or other flavourless oil

2 dessertspoons white wine vinegar

3 oz (75 g) fresh spinach leaves

1½ oz (40 g) fresh watercress leaves

1½ oz (40 g) fresh flat-leaf parsley leaves

2 tablespoons chopped fresh tarragon

1 tablespoon snipped fresh chives

1 tablespoon lemon juice or more, to taste

salt and freshly milled black pepper

The way I cook a salmon is extremely slowly, wrapped in foil in the oven. I cannot recommend this method highly enough. With skin and bones, head and tail intact, there is not only a captured concentration of flavours, but also a guaranteed succulent moistness that no other cooking method can produce. The best accompaniment is a sweet, very green mayonnaise with summer herbs, which I think is best made the day before, if possible, to allow the flavours to develop.

First, make the mayonnaise. Break the whole eggs straight into the goblet of a blender or food processor, sprinkle in the mustard powder and add the garlic clove and 1 teaspoon salt. Measure the oil into a jug, then switch the machine on. To blend everything thoroughly, pour the oil in a thin, very steady trickle with the motor running. You must be very careful here – too much oil in too soon means the sauce will curdle. When all the oil is in, add the white wine vinegar and blend. Then switch off and season to taste with salt and black pepper.

Now rinse the spinach, watercress and parsley under cold water and put these into a medium saucepan. With the heat turned to medium, stir the leaves around until everything has just wilted, then tip them into a colander and rinse under cold water to keep the colour. Now squeeze out the excess moisture very carefully, thoroughly pressing and squeezing with a wooden spoon. Then transfer the cooked leaves to the mayonnaise with the chopped tarragon and chives and whiz until smooth and green. There will be some fine specks but that's okay. Now do a bit of tasting and season with lemon juice, salt and pepper.

When you are ready to cook the salmon, pre-heat the oven to 250°F (130°C). Start by wiping the fish with some damp kitchen paper, then place it in the centre of a large double sheet of foil, generously buttered. Put half the butter, the onion slices, bay leaves and tarragon sprigs into the centre cavity of the fish, along with a seasoning of pepper and salt. The rest of the butter should be smeared on top. Now wrap the foil over the salmon to make a loose but tightly sealed parcel. Then place the foil parcel on a large baking sheet, diagonally, so that it fits in the oven. If it seems a bit long, bend the tail end upwards and then bake in the centre of the oven for 2½ hours.

After the 2½ hours, remove the salmon from the oven and allow it to cool completely before serving. (It's best not to open the foil.) To serve, the skin will come off very easily if you first make a horizontal slit all along the middle of the salmon. Then just ease the fillets away from the bone. Serve with the sauce, some crisp, dressed salad leaves, such as Cos lettuce, and cucumber, and hot buttered new potatoes or potato salad.

Note For other weights of salmon, the cooking times are: for 2 lb (900 g) 1½ hours; for 3 lb (1.35 kg) 2 hours; for 5 lb (2.25 kg) 3 hours. Unfortunately, the gas equivalent of 250°F (130°C), which used to be gas mark ½, no longer exists. So, if you use a modern gas cooker that begins at gas mark 1, give the fish you are using 25 minutes' less cooking time.

Note This recipe contains raw eggs.

Salmon in Champagne Sauce
Serves 6

6 middle-cut fillets of salmon
(6-7 oz/175-200g each)

9 fl oz (250 ml) Champagne

¾ oz (20 g) butter, plus a little extra
for greasing

2 medium shallots, finely chopped

¾ oz (20 g) plain flour

7 fl oz (200 ml) double cream

6 teaspoons keta (salmon caviar),
to serve

salt and freshly milled
black pepper

You will also need a large,
deep frying pan with a lid
(10 inches/25.5 cm) or a sauté
pan, to hold the salmon fillets
in one layer.

I was served this memorable recipe at a house of a Champagne producer in Rheims and this is my version.

First of all, smear a little butter over the base of the frying pan, then arrange the fillets in it. Now slowly pour the Champagne over the salmon (it will foam quite a lot but not to worry), then bring it to a simmer over a medium heat. Because they're not going to be quite submerged, spoon the Champagne over the top of the fish before putting the lid on. Then gently poach the salmon for about 8-10 minutes. The tip of a knife inserted into the thickest part will show if it is cooked when you just ease the flesh back.

While the salmon is poaching, melt the butter in a medium saucepan and cook the shallots in it over a gentle heat for 5-6 minutes until softened and golden but not browned. When the salmon is cooked, carefully lift the fillets into a warmed dish, cover them with foil and keep warm. Next, add the flour to the buttery shallot juices, stir it in and cook for 1-2 minutes more. Now gradually add the salmon poaching liquid to the pan, a little at a time, then blend in the double cream, whisking until the sauce is smooth. Let it come to a simmer and cook for 1-2 minutes, then taste and add some seasoning.

Serve the salmon fillets on warmed plates with a little of the sauce spooned over and a teaspoon of keta on top, and hand the rest of the sauce around in a warmed jug. I think steamed Anya potatoes tossed in butter and chives are a nice accompaniment, perhaps with fresh, shelled peas, or a green salad with plenty of cucumber and a lemony dressing.

Chilled Marinated Trout with Fennel
Serves 2

2 rainbow trout (8 oz/225 g each)

1 bulb fennel, trimmed and sliced (green tops reserved)

¾ teaspoon whole black peppercorns

¾ teaspoon coriander seeds

½ teaspoon fennel seeds

2 tablespoons extra virgin olive oil

1 clove garlic, finely chopped

1 small onion, finely chopped

1 lb (450 g) ripe, red tomatoes, skinned and chopped

1 tablespoon lemon juice

1 tablespoon white wine vinegar

8 fl oz (225 ml) dry white wine

½ teaspoon fresh oregano

salt and freshly milled black pepper

For the garnish

2 small spring onions, finely chopped

2 tablespoons chopped fresh parsley

grated zest of 1 lemon

fennel tops (see above)

This makes a very appropriate main course for a warm day. It's a doddle to prepare and it has the advantage of being cooked and left to marinate, so that when the time comes you have literally nothing to do but serve it. We like this either with a plain mixed leaf salad or, if the weather's chilly, served warm with tiny new potatoes and a leafy salad.

Begin by washing the fish in cold water and drying them with kitchen paper. Then warm a large frying pan (10 inches/25.5 cm) over a gentle heat, crush the peppercorns, coriander and fennel seeds in a mortar, add them to the pan and let them dry-roast for about 1 minute to draw out the flavours. Then add the olive oil, garlic and onion and let them cook gently for about 5 minutes or until the onion is pale gold.

Next, add the tomatoes, lemon juice, wine vinegar and white wine, stir and, when it begins to bubble, season with salt and pepper and add the oregano. Now add the sliced fennel to the pan, followed by the trout, basting the fish with the juices. Put a timer on and give the whole thing 10 minutes' gentle simmering. After that, use a fish slice and fork to turn each fish over carefully on to its other side – don't prod it or anything like that, or the flesh will break. Then give it another 10 minutes' cooking on the other side. Gently remove the trout to a shallow serving dish, spoon the sauce all over, cool, cover with clingfilm and leave them in a cool place.

If you want to make this dish the day before, that's okay, provided you keep it refrigerated and remove it an hour before serving. Either way, sprinkle each trout with the garnish (made by simply combining all the ingredients together) before taking them to the table.

Seared Spiced Salmon Steaks with Black Bean Salsa
Serves 6

6 salmon steaks
(5-6 oz/150-175 g each)

3 fat cloves garlic

2 teaspoons sea salt

1½ inch (4 cm) piece
of root ginger, grated

grated zest of 2 limes
(reserve the juice for the salsa)

a good pinch of ground cinnamon

a good pinch of ground cumin

2 tablespoons light olive oil

½ oz (10 g) fresh coriander leaves
(reserve 6 sprigs and finely chop
the remainder)

freshly milled black pepper

For the salsa

4 oz (110 g) black beans soaked
overnight in twice their volume of
cold water

12 oz (350 g) ripe but firm
tomatoes, skinned, deseeded and
finely chopped

1 red chilli, deseeded and finely
chopped

½ oz (10 g) fresh coriander leaves,
finely chopped

1 medium red onion,
finely chopped

1 tablespoon extra virgin olive oil

juice of 2 limes (see above)

½ teaspoon salt

You will also need a solid
baking sheet.

Everyone I know who has eaten this has loved it. The black bean salsa looks very pretty alongside the salmon and provides a marvellous contrast of flavours and textures, and what's more, the whole thing is so little trouble to prepare.

A few hours before you want to cook the salmon, wipe each of the steaks with damp kitchen paper and remove any visible bones, using tweezers. Place the salmon on a plate, then, with a pestle and mortar, crush the garlic cloves and sea salt together until you have a creamy purée. Now add the grated ginger, lime zest, cinnamon and cumin, 1 tablespoon of the light olive oil and the chopped coriander, and a good grinding of black pepper. Mix everything together and spread a little of this mixture on each salmon steak. Cover with clingfilm and set aside for the flavours to develop and permeate the salmon.

To make the salsa, drain and rinse the beans in plenty of cold water, put them in a saucepan with enough water to cover, bring to the boil and boil rapidly for 10 minutes. Then reduce the heat and simmer the beans for 30 minutes until tender. Drain and allow them to cool completely before adding all the other ingredients. Then leave them, covered, for several hours to allow the flavours to develop.

When you're ready to cook the salmon, pre-heat the grill to its highest setting. Brush the baking sheet with the remaining light olive oil and put it under the grill to heat up. When the grill is really hot, remove the baking sheet, using an oven glove, and place the salmon pieces on it. They will sear and sizzle as they touch the hot metal. Position the tray 3 inches (7.5 cm) from the heat and grill them for 7 minutes exactly. Use a kitchen timer, as the timing is vital.

Remove them when the time is up and use a sharp knife to ease the skins off. Transfer to warm plates and garnish with the reserved sprigs of coriander. Serve immediately with the black bean salsa.

Salmon Coulibiac
Serves 6

1 lb 4 oz (570 g) salmon tail fillet, skinned

3 oz (75 g) butter

3 oz (75 g) white basmati rice

8 fl oz (225 ml) fish stock

1 medium onion, finely chopped

4 oz (110 g) small button mushrooms, finely sliced

1 tablespoon chopped fresh dill

1 teaspoon lemon zest

2 tablespoons fresh lemon juice

2 large eggs, hard-boiled and roughly chopped

1½ tablespoons chopped fresh parsley

salt and freshly milled black pepper

For the pastry

a 375 g pack of fresh, ready-rolled puff pastry

1 oz (25 g) butter, melted

1 egg, lightly beaten

flour for dusting

You will also need a solid baking tray, 12 x 16 inches (30 x 40 cm), and a lattice cutter.

Pre-heat the oven to gas mark 4, 350°F (180°C).

This is one of the best fish pies ever invented. Serve it in slices with some Foaming Hollandaise sauce (see page 126) and a mixed-leaf salad tossed in a lemony dressing.

First of all, melt 1 oz (25 g) of the butter in a medium saucepan and stir in the rice. Then, when the rice is coated with butter, add the stock and a little salt and bring it up to simmering point, then stir well and cover with a lid. Cook the rice for 15 minutes exactly, then take the pan off the heat, remove the lid and allow it to cool. As soon as the rice is cooking, take a sheet of buttered foil, lay the salmon on it and add some seasoning. Then wrap it up loosely, pleating the foil at the top and folding in the edges. Place it on a baking sheet and pop it in the oven for just 10 minutes – the salmon needs to be only half cooked. After that, remove it from the oven, open the foil and allow it to cool.

Now, while the salmon and the rice are cooling, melt the remaining 2 oz (50 g) of butter in a small saucepan and gently sweat the onion in it for about 10 minutes until it softens. Then add the mushrooms and half the dill, and carry on cooking gently for a further 5 minutes. Now stir in the lemon zest and juice, some salt and black pepper, and allow this mixture to cool. Next, take a large bowl and combine the salmon, broken up into large flakes, the eggs, the remaining dill and half the parsley and give all this a good seasoning. Next, in another bowl, combine the rice mixture with the onion, mushrooms and the rest of the parsley, giving this some seasoning, too.

Now for the pastry. What you need to do here is, unfold it and place it lengthways on a lightly floured surface, then, using a tape measure, roll the pastry into a 14 inch (35 cm) square. Then cut it into two lengths, one 6½ inches (16 cm) and one 7½ inches (19 cm).

Now lightly brush the baking sheet and surface of the pastry with some of the melted butter and lay the narrower strip of pastry on to it. First, spoon half the rice mixture along the centre leaving a gap of at least 1 inch (2.5 cm) all the way round. Next, spoon the salmon mixture on top of the rice, building it up as high as possible and pressing and moulding it with your hands – what you're aiming for is a loaf shape of mixture. Then lightly mould the rest of the rice mixture on top of the salmon and brush the 1 inch (2.5 cm) border all round with beaten egg. Next, take the lattice cutter and run it along the centre of the other piece of pastry, leaving an even margin of about 1 inch (2.5 cm) all round. Brush the surface of the pastry with melted butter, then very carefully lift this and cover the salmon mixture with it. The idea here is not to let the lattice open too much as you lift it, because it will open naturally as it goes over the filling. Press the edges together all round to seal, then trim the pastry so that you're left with a ¾ inch (2 cm) border.

Now, using the back edge of a knife, knock up the edges of the pastry, then crimp it all along using your thumb and the back of the knife, pulling the knife towards the filling each time as you go round. Alternatively, just fork it all around.

When you're ready to cook the coulibiac, raise the oven temperature to gas mark 7, 425°F (220°C) and brush all over the pastry with beaten egg and any remaining butter. And, if you feel like it, you can re-roll some of the trimmings and cut out little fish shapes to decorate the top. Now place the coulibiac on to the high shelf of the oven and bake it for 20-25 minutes until it's golden brown. Remove it from the oven and leave it to rest for about 10 minutes before cutting into slices.

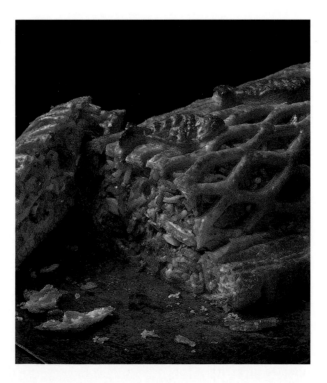

Salmon Fish Cakes
with Cucumber and Dill Sauce
Makes 12 (serves 3-4)

For the fish cakes

a 418 g tin of red salmon

10 oz (275 g) Desirée or King
Edward potatoes, peeled
and quartered

2 tablespoons mayonnaise

2 heaped tablespoons chopped
fresh parsley

2 heaped tablespoons capers,
rinsed, patted dry and chopped

6 cornichons, drained and chopped

2 large eggs, hard-boiled and chopped

1 dessertspoon anchovy paste
or 4 anchovies, mashed up

2 tablespoons lemon juice

¼ teaspoon powdered mace

¼ teaspoon cayenne pepper

salt and freshly milled
black pepper

For the cucumber and dill sauce

1 lb (450 g) cucumber

1 tablespoon chopped fresh dill,
plus a few sprigs to garnish

1 oz (25 g) butter

2½ fl oz (65 ml) crème fraîche

a little lemon juice

For the coating and frying

1 large egg, beaten

3 oz (75 g) matzo meal or fresh
white breadcrumbs

2 tablespoons groundnut or other
flavourless oil

½ oz (10 g) butter

This combines salmon and creamy potato in a crisp coating, with a light summery sauce.

First, steam the potatoes with a dessertspoon of salt for 25 minutes or until they are absolutely tender. Then remove them from the steamer, drain off the water, return them to the pan and cover with a clean tea cloth to absorb some of the steam for about 5 minutes. Now mash them to a purée with the mayonnaise, using an electric hand whisk, then add some seasoning. Now, in a large mixing bowl, simply combine all the ingredients for the fish cakes together. Mix really thoroughly, then season again if it needs it. After that, cover the bowl and place it in the fridge, giving it about 2 hours to chill and become firm.

To make the sauce: first pare off the peel of the cucumber with a potato peeler, as thinly as possible, as the green bit just beneath the surface of the peel is important for the colour of the sauce. Then cut the cucumber in half lengthways and remove the seeds, using a teaspoon. Now cut the cucumber into ¼ inch (5 mm) dice. Next, heat the butter in a smallish pan over a very low heat, add the diced cucumber and some salt and toss it around in the butter. Then put a lid on and, keeping the heat as low as possible, let the cucumber sweat gently for about 10 minutes, shaking the pan from time to time to make sure none of it catches on the base. As soon as the pieces of cucumber are just tender, stir in the crème fraîche, dill and a little lemon juice. Season with more salt if it needs it and some black pepper, then warm gently. Now tip half the sauce into a blender or food processor, whiz until it's smooth, then mix together with the rest of the sauce and set aside.

When you are ready to cook the fish cakes, lightly flour a working surface, then turn the fish mixture on to it and, using your hands, pat and shape it into a long roll, 2-2½ inches (5-6 cm) in diameter. Now cut the roll into 12 round fish cakes – pat each one into a neat, flat shape and then dip them, one by one, first into beaten egg and then into the matzo meal or breadcrumbs, making sure they get a nice even coating all round.

Now, in a large frying pan heat the oil and butter over a high heat and, when it is really hot, add half the fish cakes, then turn the heat down to medium and give them 4 minutes' frying on each side. Then repeat with the other half, draining them on crumpled greaseproof paper. Serve on hot plates with the warm sauce and a sprig of dill.

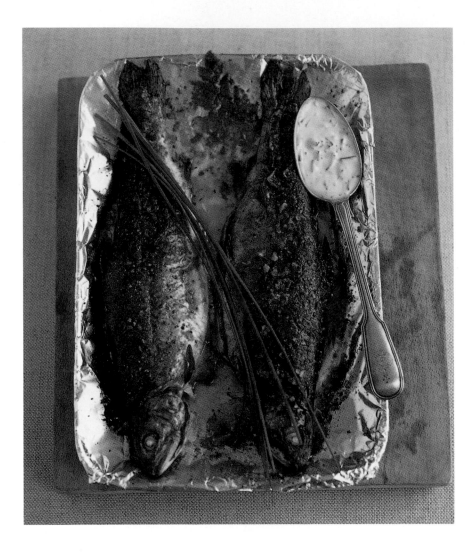

Trout with Butter, Crème Fraîche and Chives
Serves 2

2 rainbow trout
(6–7 oz/175-200 g each)

1 oz (25 g) butter, plus a little extra, melted, for brushing foil and the trout

3 fl oz (75 ml) crème fraîche

1 bay leaf

2 tablespoons snipped fresh chives

salt and freshly milled black pepper

You will also need a small roasting tin, lined with foil.

Pre-heat the oven to gas mark 7, 425°F (220°C).

This recipe is a good one for anyone who has to work and then prepare a meal quickly – the whole thing takes less than 30 minutes.

First, brush the foil in the roasting tin with a little melted butter. Then wash the trout in cold water and dry them very thoroughly. Now place them in the roasting tin, brush each one with a little melted butter and season with salt and pepper. Bake them, on a high shelf in the oven, for about 10-15 minutes.

While that's happening, pour the crème fraîche into a saucepan, add the bay leaf and bring it up to simmering point. Then remove the bay leaf and stir in the chives and 1 oz (25 g) butter, season with salt and pepper, and pour this mixture into a warm jug. Serve it with the fish, some buttered new potatoes and a green salad or some fresh, cooked spinach.

Roasted Salmon Fillets with a Crusted Pecorino and Pesto Topping
Serves 2

2 skinless salmon fillets
(5-6 oz/150-175 g each, and about
¾ inch/2 cm thick)

1 rounded tablespoon finely grated
Pecorino cheese

2 tablespoons fresh pesto sauce

juice of ½ lemon

2 tablespoons fresh breadcrumbs

salt and freshly milled
black pepper

You will also need a baking tray,
10 x 14 inches (25.5 x 35 cm),
lined with foil and lightly oiled.

Pre-heat the oven to gas mark 8,
450°F (230°C).

This recipe, given to me by my friend Lin Cooper, has proved to be one of the most popular fish recipes I've ever published. The combination of fresh pesto sauce with all its bold Italian flavours and fresh salmon is sublime, and that's not all – the whole thing takes about 15 minutes from start to finish.

Begin by trimming the fillets, if needed, and run your hand over the surface of the fish to check that there aren't any stray bones lurking. Now place the fish on the prepared baking tray and give each one a good squeeze of lemon juice and a seasoning of salt and pepper. Next, give the pesto a good stir and measure 2 tablespoons into a small bowl, mix one-third of the breadcrumbs with it to form a paste and spread this over both fish fillets. Then, mix half the cheese with the remaining breadcrumbs and scatter this over the pesto, then finish off with the remaining cheese.

Now place the baking tray on the middle shelf of the oven and cook for 10 minutes, by which time the top should be golden brown and crispy and the salmon just cooked and moist. Serve with steamed new potatoes.

Steamed Trout Fillets in Lettuce Parcels with a Thai Stuffing

Serves 2 as a main course or 4 as a starter

4 skinless trout fillets
(3-4 oz/75-110 g each)

8 large lettuce leaves
from a round lettuce

For the stuffing

1 tablespoon groundnut or other flavourless oil

2 spring onions, finely chopped, (including the green parts)

2 cloves garlic, crushed

grated zest and juice of 1 lime

1 rounded dessertspoon freshly grated ginger

1 rounded tablespoon grated creamed coconut

½ oz (10 g) fresh coriander (reserve a few sprigs for garnish and chop remaining leaves)

salt and freshly milled black pepper

To serve

1 lime, quartered

a few sprigs of fresh coriander (see above)

You will also need a large saucepan and a fan steamer.

This is an extremely simple, extremely quick recipe that tastes positively five star. You won't believe how easy it is. If you want to prepare it a couple of hours in advance, wrap the stuffed fillets in foil, keep them in the fridge and just wrap the lettuce leaves round before steaming. You can use sole or plaice instead of trout.

To make the Thai stuffing, heat the oil in a small pan and gently sauté the spring onions and garlic for just 30 seconds. Then remove the pan from the heat and stir in the rest of the stuffing ingredients. (If you want to make this ahead of time, make sure the stuffing is absolutely cold before using it to fill the fish.)

Now lay the fillets on a work surface, skinned side uppermost. Season each fillet, then, using a small palette knife, spread an equal amount of the stuffing along the length of each one. Now fold each fillet by tucking the thin end to the centre and the thicker end on top of that to form a neat parcel.

Next, place the lettuce leaves in a bowl and pour some boiling water from the kettle over them. Then lift them straight out, using a draining spoon, and pat them dry with kitchen paper. They will now be really flexible and you can fold them around each fillet very easily, using 2 leaves for each. Fold and wrap them round securely so as not to lose any of the filling. Place the parcels in the steamer over boiling water, cover with a lid and time them for exactly 8 minutes. Serve, garnished with sprigs of coriander and lime quarters to squeeze over. For a main course, serve with Thai fragrant rice mixed with some sautéed desiccated coconut.

Salmon with a Saffron Couscous Crust and Tomato and Olive Vinaigrette
Serves 4

4 skinless salmon fillets (5 oz/150 g each)

2-3 good pinches of saffron stamens

5 oz (150 g) couscous

7 fl oz (200 ml) dry white wine

1 large egg, beaten

salt and freshly milled black pepper

For the tomato and olive vinaigrette

8 oz (225 g) tomatoes, skinned, deseeded and chopped small

3 oz (75 g) pitted black olives, chopped to the same size as the tomatoes

1 fat clove garlic

1 teaspoon wholegrain mustard

1 tablespoon white wine vinegar

1 tablespoon lemon juice

4 fl oz (120 ml) olive oil

1 tablespoon chopped fresh chervil or flat-leaf parsley

sea salt and freshly milled black pepper

Pre-heat the oven to gas mark 5, 375°F (190°C).

This is unusual but works like a dream and is very simple to prepare. The couscous crust encases the salmon and keeps all the fragrant juices inside intact. Served with perhaps some fresh, shelled peas, it makes a perfect main course for summer entertaining.

First of all, prepare the couscous – which is dead simple. All you do is place it in a bowl, then heat up the wine till just at simmering point, whisk the saffron into it, along with some salt and pepper, and pour the whole lot over the couscous grains. Then leave the couscous on one side until it has absorbed all the liquid. After this, fluff it by making cutting movements across and through it with a knife.

Now take each salmon fillet, season with salt and pepper, and dip it first into beaten egg, then sit it on top of the couscous and, using your hands, coat it on all sides, pressing the couscous evenly all round (it works in just the same way as breadcrumbs). Now place the coated fillets on a lightly greased baking sheet and, if you want, cover with clingfilm and keep refrigerated until they're needed.

To make the vinaigrette, crush the garlic with 1 teaspoon of sea salt, using a pestle and mortar, then add the mustard, vinegar, lemon juice, olive oil and a good seasoning of black pepper, and whisk thoroughly. About half an hour before serving, add the tomatoes, olives and chopped chervil or flat-leaf parsley.

When you are ready to cook the salmon fillets, pop them into the pre-heated oven and bake for 15-20 minutes, or a little longer if the fish is very thick. Serve each one in a pool of Tomato and Olive Vinaigrette, and hand round the rest of the vinaigrette separately.

Teriyaki Grilled Marinated Salmon with Marinated Cucumber and Sesame Salad
Serves 4

4 skinless salmon fillets
(5 oz /150 g each)

½ teaspoon groundnut or other flavourless oil for greasing

a few snipped fresh chives, to garnish

For the marinade

4 tablespoons each Japanese soy sauce, sake (Japanese rice wine) and mirin (Japanese sweet rice wine)

1 teaspoon golden caster sugar

1 tablespoon peeled and grated fresh root ginger

2 fat cloves garlic, crushed

For the salad

1 cucumber

2 tablespoons sesame seeds

3 tablespoons Japanese soy sauce

2 teaspoons each sake, mirin and rice vinegar

1 teaspoon golden caster sugar

You will also need a large baking tray.

I'm using salmon here, which works best, but it can be made with other fish, such as cod or haddock fillet, too.

To begin with, make the marinade. All you do is whisk together the soy sauce, sake, mirin, sugar, ginger and garlic. Next, place the salmon fillets in a small, shallow dish and pour the marinade over. Now cover them and leave in a cool place for 2 hours, turning them once, halfway through the marinating time.

To make the cucumber salad, begin by toasting the sesame seeds. Do this by pre-heating a medium, heavy-based frying pan over a medium heat, then add the sesame seeds, moving them around in the pan to brown evenly. As soon as they begin to splutter and pop and turn golden, they're ready. This will take 1-2 minutes. Then remove them to a plate. Next, cut the cucumber in half, then into quarters and then into eighths (all lengthways). Remove the seeds, then chop each piece on the diagonal into 3 inch (7.5 cm) strips and place them in a bowl. After that, measure the soy sauce, sake, mirin, vinegar and sugar into a screw-top jar, shake them together thoroughly, then pour this mixture over the cucumber wedges and leave them to marinate for about an hour – again, giving them one good stir at half-time.

When you're ready to cook the salmon, pre-heat the grill to its highest setting for at least 10 minutes. Brush the baking tray with the oil and put it under the grill to pre-heat as well. When the grill is really hot, remove the tray, using a thick oven glove. Now take the salmon steaks out of the marinade (reserving it) and shake them slightly before placing them on to the baking tray. (They should sear and sizzle as they touch the hot metal.) Then position the tray about 3 inches (7.5 cm) from the heat source and grill them for 6 minutes exactly. I advise you to use a kitchen timer here, as the timing is pretty crucial. Meanwhile, pour the marinade into a small pan and bring it up to simmering point, allowing it to bubble, until the mixture has reduced by about a third, or until it is syrupy. Strain this sauce through a sieve. Serve the salmon with the sauce poured over, garnished with the chives. Sprinkle the sesame seeds over the cucumber salad and hand it round separately on a plate.

Oily & Other Fish

Barbecued Sardines with Summer Herb Sauce
Serves 4

2 lb (900 g) fresh sardines (about 12)

6 oz (175 g) fresh sorrel leaves (stalks removed), washed and dried

about 2 tablespoons olive oil

salt and freshly milled black pepper

For the sauce

1 rounded tablespoon snipped fresh chives

1 tablespoon chopped fresh tarragon

1 rounded tablespoon chopped fresh basil

1 rounded tablespoon chopped fresh flat-leaf parsley or chervil

3 shallots, finely chopped

1 large clove garlic, finely chopped

3 tablespoons cider vinegar

2 teaspoons balsamic vinegar

salt and freshly milled black pepper

Sardines have a very evocative flavour and aroma that suit eating out of doors perfectly. This is a recipe that can easily be prepared well ahead of time and, if the coals on the barbecue are good and hot, the fish are cooked in moments. If sorrel is unavailable, use young spinach leaves mixed with some grated zest of lemon – about 1 tablespoon – for the stuffing. If it rains, the sardines will cook perfectly well under a domestic grill or on a ridged grill pan.

First, prepare the sardines. Use a small pair of scissors to cut open the bellies and remove the innards. Then wipe them inside and out with damp kitchen paper and arrange them on a plate. Next, chop the sorrel leaves fairly finely, then season and use three-quarters of them to stuff inside the bellies of the fish. Sprinkle the oil over the fish and rub it in so that they all get a good coating.

Now prepare the sauce by placing the remaining sorrel leaves, along with the other herbs, the shallots and garlic in a jug or serving bowl and add 5 tablespoons of boiling water, followed by the vinegars. Stir well and season with salt and pepper.

The sardines will need very little time to cook – just 2 minutes on each side. Serve with the sauce handed round separately.

Fried Herrings with Oatmeal and a Beetroot Relish
Serves 2

2 medium herrings (10-12 oz/ 275-350 g each when whole), boned (see page 125)

3 oz (75 g) coarse oatmeal

2 heaped tablespoons seasoned plain flour

1 large egg, beaten

2 tablespoons lard or flavourless oil

salt and freshly milled black pepper

For the beetroot relish

6 oz (175 g) cooked beetroot, chopped into ¼ inch (5 mm) dice

2 shallots, finely chopped

4 cornichons, drained and finely chopped

1 heaped tablespoon salted capers, rinsed and drained

1 dessertspoon red wine vinegar

1 dessertspoon good-quality mayonnaise

a little chopped fresh parsley, to serve

salt and freshly milled black pepper

To garnish

a few sprigs of fresh flat-leaf parsley

a few lime wedges

Why is it that fresh sardines are so highly thought of and yet herrings are largely ignored? Firstly, they're very closely related, so their taste is similar; secondly, herrings don't have to be imported and therefore are fresh, plump and bright, and, being larger, they have more lovely, juicy flesh. Any leftover beetroot relish can be kept in the fridge for a couple of days.

Begin by making the beetroot relish and, to do this, simply mix all the ingredients together and sprinkle with the chopped parsley.

Now wipe the herrings with kitchen paper, then place them flesh side up on a plate and season well. Dip both sides into the seasoned flour, then dip the flesh side only into first the beaten egg, then the oatmeal, pressing it down firmly into their flesh. Now heat the lard or oil in a large frying pan (10 inches/25.5 cm) over a high heat until it's shimmering hot, then fry the herrings flesh side (oatmeal side) down for 2-3 minutes, or until they look golden and crusty when you lift them a little with a spatula. Now flip them over, using a spatula and fork, and let them cook for another 1-2 minutes, then transfer them to crumpled greaseproof or kitchen paper to drain before serving with the relish and some waxy potatoes. Garnish with the parsley and lime wedges.

Herrings with Caper Stuffing
Serves 4

4 herrings (about 8 oz/225 g each), gutted

1 oz (25 g) butter

For the stuffing

3 oz (75 g) fresh white breadcrumbs

1 teaspoon mustard powder

3 tablespoons finely chopped parsley

zest of 1 lemon, finely grated

juice of ½ lemon

1 tablespoon capers, rinsed, patted dry and chopped

1 oz (25 g) butter

1 medium onion, finely chopped

salt and freshly milled black pepper

You will also need string to tie the herrings and a well-buttered, shallow baking dish.

Pre-heat the oven to gas mark 7, 425°F (220°C).

You can, if you are lucky, buy herring fillets for this recipe. If not, boning is quite easy (see page 125).

To make the stuffing, first mix the breadcrumbs, mustard powder, parsley, lemon zest and juice, and capers together in a large mixing bowl. Now heat the butter in a frying pan and soften the onion in it over a low heat for 10 minutes, before adding it, together with its buttery juices, to the breadcrumb mixture and seasoning everything with salt and freshly milled black pepper.

Now open each herring out flat, and spread a quarter of the stuffing down one side of each one, then fold the other side back to its original shape. Using string, tie a short length in three places around each fish to stop the filling from falling out while the herrings are cooking.

Then put the fish in the buttered baking dish, place a knob of butter on each one and bake near the top of the oven for 15 minutes, basting once with the buttery juice.

Chargrilled Tuna with Warm Coriander and Caper Vinaigrette
Serves 2

2 tuna steaks
(about 8 oz/225 g each)

1 tablespoon extra virgin olive oil

salt and freshly milled
black pepper

For the vinaigrette

1 heaped tablespoon roughly
chopped fresh coriander leaves

1 heaped tablespoon salted
capers, rinsed and patted dry

grated zest and juice 1 lime

1 tablespoon white wine vinegar

1 clove garlic, finely chopped

1 shallot, finely chopped

1 heaped teaspoon wholegrain
mustard

2 tablespoons extra virgin olive oil

salt and freshly milled
black pepper

You will also need a cast-iron
ridged griddle.

Because domestic grills are so variable in their efficiency, I think a ridged griddle is a very good investment. It's particularly good for thick tuna steaks and gives those lovely charred stripes that look so attractive.

First of all, brush the grill pan with a little of the olive oil, then place it over a very high heat and let it pre-heat till very hot – about 10 minutes. Meanwhile, wipe the fish steaks with kitchen paper, then place them on a plate, brush them with the remaining olive oil and season both sides with salt and black pepper. When the grill pan is ready, place the tuna steaks on it and give them about 2 minutes on each side.

Meanwhile, make the vinaigrette by placing all the ingredients in a small saucepan and whisking them together over a gentle heat – no actual cooking is needed here; all this needs is to be warm.

When the tuna steaks are ready, remove them to warm serving plates, pour over the vinaigrette and serve with steamed new potatoes.

Greek-style Squid
with Lemon, Garlic and Olive Oil
Serves 2

1 lb (450 g) small squid,
cleaned and prepared
(see recipe)

grated zest and juice
of 1 large lemon

3 cloves garlic, finely chopped

3 fl oz (75 ml) olive oil,
preferably Greek

2 heaped tablespoons chopped
fresh parsley

lemon wedges,
to squeeze over

salt and freshly milled
black pepper

Close your eyes when you eat your first mouthful of this one and in your mind you'll be right there on some lovely Greek island – it's one of those very simple things that also tastes extremely special. It's easy, too, as the squid is all prepared for you, so the whole thing takes no longer than 15 minutes from start to finish.

All you do with the squid is pull out the little tentacles and wash them, dry with kitchen paper, and reserve them. Next, cut the body section into ½ inch (1 cm) rings and wash them under cold running water, then pat dry with kitchen paper. Place them in a shallow dish, adding the reserved tentacles. Squeeze the lemon juice over, toss and leave it for 5 minutes, when it will have absorbed most of the juice. Drain the squid through a colander and shake to remove excess liquid.

Next, heat the oil in a large, solid frying pan, add the garlic and lemon zest, cooking very slowly as the oil heats up. When it is really hot, add the squid and fry it in the hot oil, keeping it on the move so it just slightly takes on colour at the edges – it will only take about 1-2 minutes to cook.

Then add the seasoning and parsley and serve it straightaway from the pan, with lemon wedges to squeeze over. This is particularly good served with a green salad and some warm pitta bread to dip into the luscious juices.

Linguine with Sardines, Chilli and Capers
Serves 2

8 oz (225 g) dried linguine

a 120 g tin of sardines in olive oil, well drained and the fish flaked into bite-sized pieces

1 tablespoon sardine oil, reserved from the tin for frying

1 red chilli, deseeded and finely chopped

1 tablespoon salted capers, rinsed and patted dry

1 clove garlic, chopped

7 oz (200 g) tinned Italian chopped tomatoes, well drained, or 4 medium, ripe tomatoes, skinned and diced

a few fresh basil leaves, roughly torn, to garnish

salt and freshly milled black pepper

Good old tinned sardines are fashionable again and are an ideal storecupboard ingredient – great for serving on toast sprinkled with a little balsamic vinegar and lots of seasoning. This is also the perfect storecupboard meal for two, made in moments and good for students or anyone on a tight budget. I love the shape of linguine, but any pasta can be used.

First of all, you need to cook the pasta. Always use a large cooking pot and make sure you have at least 4 pints (2.25 litres) of water for every 8 oz (225 g) of pasta and 1 tablespoon of salt. Bring the water up to a good fierce boil before the pasta goes in and cook it for 8-12 minutes without a lid, until *al dente*.

Meanwhile, heat the tablespoon of sardine oil in a small frying pan, fry the garlic and chilli for about 4 minutes, until softened, then add the tomatoes, sardines and capers and gently heat them through, stirring occasionally. Taste and season with salt and black pepper.

When the pasta is ready, drain it into a colander, then quickly return it to the saucepan. Add the sauce, toss it around thoroughly for 30 seconds or so, then serve in hot pasta bowls with the torn basil sprinkled over.

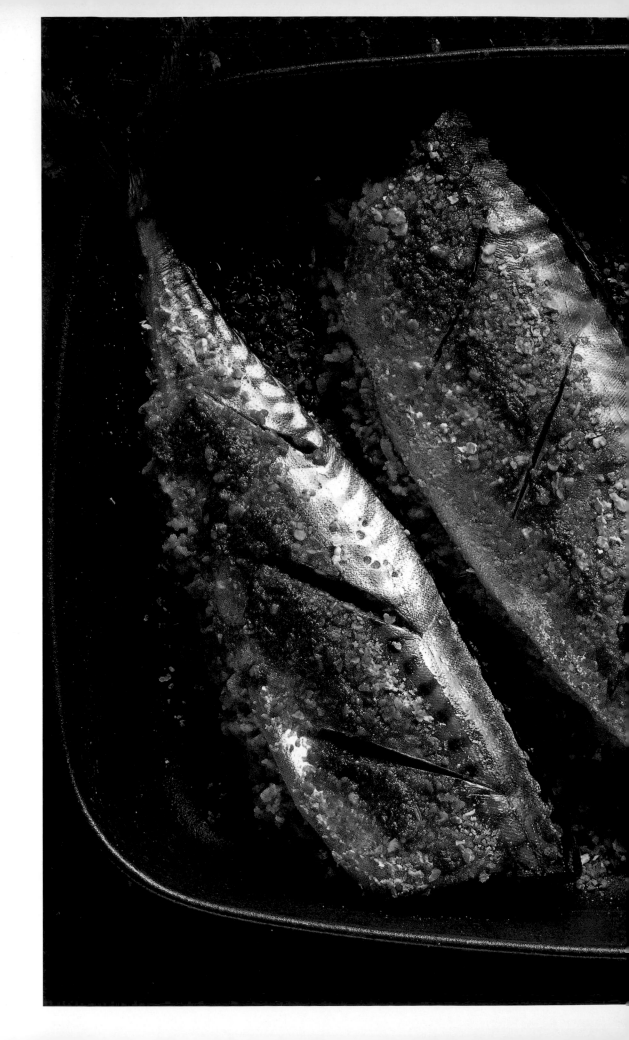

Oven-baked Mackerel Stuffed with Pesto Mash
Serves 4

4 mackerel (10 oz/275 g each), heads removed

12 oz (350 g) Desirée potatoes, peeled and cut into evenly sized pieces

6 spring onions, finely chopped (including the green parts)

1 oz (25 g) brown bread (about 1½ slices), cubed

1 tablespoon rolled oats

1 dessertspoon olive oil, plus a little for brushing

salt and freshly milled black pepper

For the pesto sauce

2 oz (50 g) fresh basil leaves

1 large clove garlic, crushed

1 tablespoon pine nuts

6 tablespoons extra virgin olive oil

1 oz (25 g) Pecorino Romano, grated

salt

To serve

lemon quarters

a few sprigs of fresh flat-leaf parsley

You will also need a solid baking tray, about 12 x 16 inches (30 x 40 cm), lined with kitchen foil and brushed with a little olive oil.

Pre-heat the oven to gas mark 6, 400°F (200°C).

It takes only one word to describe this recipe – wow! It's simply one of the best fish recipes ever (see picture on page 84). Easy to make and such a divine combination of flavours, it can also be prepared in advance, so all you have to do is just pop it in the oven, make a salad and a nice lemony dressing.

First, cook the potatoes in boiling, salted water for 20 minutes. Test them with a skewer and, when they're absolutely tender, drain them well. Leave them in the saucepan and cover with a clean tea cloth to absorb some of the steam. Meanwhile, make the pesto sauce. If you have a blender, put the basil, garlic, pine nuts and olive oil, together with some salt, in the goblet and blend until you have a smooth purée. Then transfer the purée to a bowl and stir in the grated Pecorino cheese. If you don't have a blender, use a large pestle and mortar to pound the basil, garlic and pine nuts to a paste. Slowly add the salt and cheese, then very gradually add the oil until you have obtained a smooth purée. Next, add all but 1 tablespoon of the pesto to the potatoes, then use an electric hand whisk to mash them – start with a slow speed to break them up, then go on to high until you have a smooth, lump-free purée. Now fold in the spring onions and taste to check the seasoning.

Next, make the topping for the fish by dropping the cubes of bread into a food processor or blender with the motor switched on, then follow with the rolled oats until all is uniformly crumbled.

To prepare the fish, wipe them inside and out with kitchen paper, lay them on the foil-lined baking tray and make three diagonal cuts about 1 inch (2.5 cm) in depth all along the top side of the mackerel. Spoon the pesto mash into the body cavities, pack it in neatly, then fork the edges of the potato to give some texture. Now brush the surface of the fish with olive oil, scatter it with the crumbs and finally, add the dessertspoon of olive oil to the remaining pesto and drizzle it over the crumbs, using a teaspoon. Now it's ready for the oven: bake for 25 minutes on a high shelf, then serve with lemon quarters and sprigs of flat-leaf parsley.

Chargrilled Squid with Chilli Jam
Serves 4 as a starter

1 lb (450 g) small squid, cleaned and prepared (see recipe)

1 dessertspoon groundnut or other flavourless oil

salt and freshly milled black pepper

rocket leaves, to serve

For the chilli jam

1½ medium, red chillies, deseeded and roughly chopped

1 lb (450 g) very ripe tomatoes

2 cloves garlic, roughly chopped

a 1 inch (2.5 cm) piece of fresh root ginger, peeled and roughly chopped

1 tablespoon Thai fish sauce

8 oz (225 g) demerara sugar

2 fl oz (55 ml) red wine vinegar

1 tablespoon balsamic vinegar

You will also need a cast-iron, ridged griddle and a 1 lb (350 ml) jar, sterilised. To sterilise the jars, they should be washed, dried and heated in a moderate oven for 5 minutes.

We always have Easter Sunday lunch at Yetman's restaurant in Norfolk and one year, we had this brilliant starter. The chilli jam will keep in the fridge for up to three months.

The chilli jam can be done well in advance. First of all, you need to roughly chop the tomatoes. (You can leave on their skins.) Then put half of them into a blender, along with the chillies, garlic, ginger and fish sauce, whiz everything to a fine purée and pour the mixture into a large saucepan. Now pulse the remaining tomatoes in the blender until just chopped, but this time not puréed. Add these to the purée in the saucepan, along with the sugar and vinegars, and slowly bring the mixture up to boiling point, stirring all the time. When the mixture reaches the boil, turn the heat down to a gentle simmer. Skim off any foam from the surface and cook gently, uncovered, for 30-40 minutes, stirring every 5 minutes to prevent the chopped tomato settling at the bottom. You will also need to scrape down the sides of the pan during the cooking so that everything cooks evenly. The mixture should reduce to half its volume. Now pour it into the hot, sterilised jar, allow it to cool and then cover and store it in the fridge. (You will need about a third of the chilli jam for this recipe.) Next, pre-heat the griddle over a high heat.

Meanwhile, prepare the squid. Slit it on one side and open it out to give two flaps (retaining the tentacles). Pat dry with kitchen paper. (It's important that you dry the squid properly, otherwise it will stew in the pan, rather than fry.) Now, using a small sharp knife, lightly score it on the inside – if you score it on the outside, it won't curl properly. Score diagonally in one direction, then do the same in the other direction, to give little diamond shapes, taking great care not to cut right through the squid.

When the pan is searing hot, lightly brush the squid and the tentacles on both sides with the oil, then season with salt and pepper. Only season the squid the moment it goes into the pan – if you do it in advance, the salt will draw out all the moisture. Now add the squid and tentacles in batches to the hot pan and cook for 1-2 minutes, turning halfway through, until lightly charred. (Be warned – the tentacles will look as though they're coming alive!) Use tongs to transfer the first batch to a warmed plate while you cook the rest. Serve warm or cold on a bed of rocket leaves, with the chilli jam drizzled over.

Fried Herring Fillets with a Lime Pepper Crust
Serves 2

2 herrings, (about 8 oz/225 g each), gutted and boned (see page 125)

2 limes

1 rounded teaspoon whole mixed peppercorns

1 rounded dessertspoon plain flour

2 tablespoons olive oil

sea salt

For me, the humble herring, once the food of the poor, is a great delicacy with all the gutsy flavours of fresh sardines but lots more juicy flesh. Now they can be bought boned and filleted and are cooked in moments. The lime and pepper crust is fragrant and slightly crunchy. Squeeze lots of lime juice over before you start eating – it cuts through the richness perfectly.

First of all, crush the peppercorns with a pestle and mortar – not too fine, so they still have some texture. Then grate the zest of the limes and add half of it to the peppercorns, then add the flour. Mix them all together and spread the mixture out on a flat plate. Wipe the herrings dry with kitchen paper and coat the flesh side with the flour-pepper mixture. Press well into the fish to give it a good coating – anything left on the plate can be used to dust the skin side lightly.

Now, in your largest frying pan, heat the oil until it is very hot and fry the herrings, flesh side down, for about 2-3 minutes. Have a peek by lifting up the edge with a fish slice – it should be golden. Then turn the fish over on to the other side and give it another 2 minutes, and drain on crumpled baking parchment before serving. Serve sprinkled with crushed sea salt, the rest of the lime zest and the limes cut into quarters to squeeze over.

Baked Mackerel with Herb Stuffing
Serves 2

2 mackerel (about 10 oz/
275 g each), gutted and boned
(see page 125)

1 oz (25 g) butter

3 large spring onions, chopped
(including the green parts)

2 oz (50 g) white breadcrumbs

grated zest of ½ lemon

2 teaspoons lemon juice

1 tablespoon chopped fresh
parsley

1 tablespoon snipped fresh chives

1 teaspoon finely chopped fresh
tarragon

½ teaspoon fresh thyme

oil for brushing the mackerel

5 oz (150 g) natural yoghurt

salt and freshly milled
black pepper

You will also need a small
roasting tin or shallow heatproof
dish, lightly oiled.

Pre-heat the oven to gas mark 5,
375°F (190°C).

Mackerel has to be really fresh, so choose fish with a bright, silvery, sparkling skin and not dull and flabby.

Start by melting the butter in a small frying pan and gently fry the chopped spring onions for about 2 minutes, then combine with the breadcrumbs, lemon zest and juice and half the whole quantity of herbs. Season well with salt and pepper and pack an equal quantity of the mixture into the belly of each fish. Brush the fish with oil and season with salt and freshly milled pepper. Place them in the tin or heatproof dish and bake in the top half of the oven for 25 minutes.

Stir the remaining herbs into the yoghurt and season with salt and freshly milled pepper. Pour over the fish and bake for 5 minutes, then serve with some buttery potatoes and a crisp green salad.

Salade Niçoise
Serves 4-6 as a light lunch

12 oz (350 g) ripe, red tomatoes

4 oz (110 g) rocket, stalks removed

½ small young cucumber, cut into smallish chunks

1 lb (450 g) new potatoes, cooked and sliced

4 oz (110 g) fine green beans, cooked

4 shallots, finely chopped

14 oz (400 g) tinned tuna fish in oil, well drained

2 large eggs, hard-boiled, peeled and quartered

2 oz (50 g) anchovy fillets

2 oz (50 g) black olives

1 tablespoon chopped fresh parsley

For the vinaigrette dressing

1 teaspoon sea salt

1 clove garlic, peeled

1 rounded teaspoon mustard powder

1 tablespoon wine or balsamic vinegar

6 tablespoons extra virgin olive oil

2 tablespoons finely chopped fresh herbs (such as chives, tarragon, parsley, basil, chervil or mint; if using fresh oregano and thyme, use just ½ teaspoon each in the mix)

freshly milled black pepper

Nothing has changed much here over the long years I've been cooking and writing recipes – this is still one of the best combinations of salad ingredients ever invented. Slick restaurants often attempt to do trendy versions with salmon, chargrilled tuna and the like, but the original reigns supreme. In Provence, lettuce was sometimes used, sometimes not, but I now like to abandon the lettuce in favour of a few rocket leaves.

To make the vinaigrette dressing, start off with a pestle and mortar. First of all, crush the flakes of sea salt to a powder, then add the peeled clove of garlic and pound them together, which will immediately bring out the garlic juices and turn it into a smooth paste. Next, add the mustard powder, work that in, then add the wine or vinegar and some black pepper and mix thoroughly until the salt dissolves. Finally, add the olive oil. Now stir the herbs into the vinaigrette – it will look rather thick but will spread itself out beautifully once you toss it into the salad. Just before you dress the salad, pour everything into a screw-top jar and shake vigorously so it's thoroughly blended.

For the salad, begin by preparing the tomatoes. Place them in a bowl, pour boiling water over them, then, after 1 minute, drain and slip off their skins (protecting your hands with a cloth, if you need to). Now cut each tomato in half and hold each half in the palm of your hand (cut side up), then turn your hand over and squeeze gently until the seeds come out; it's best to do this over a plate or bowl to catch the seeds.

Now cut each tomato into quarters. Then, in a large salad bowl, arrange the tomatoes, rocket leaves, cucumber, potatoes, beans and chopped shallots in layers, sprinkling a little of the dressing in as you go. Next, arrange chunks of tuna and egg quarters on top, then arrange the anchovies in a criss-cross pattern, followed by a scattering of olives, the chopped parsley and a final sprinkling of dressing. Now you need to serve the salad fairly promptly and, needless to say, it needs lots of warm, crusty baguette with Normandy butter to go with it.

Soused Herrings
Serves 6

6 herrings (about 8oz/225 g each), gutted and boned (see page 125)

1½ tablespoons salt

3 teaspoons made-up English mustard

2 dill gherkins

1 Spanish onion, thinly sliced

For the marinade

1 pint (570 ml) white wine vinegar

1 teaspoon whole allspice berries

1 teaspoon whole coriander seeds

½ teaspoon mustard seeds

1 dried red chilli

a few bay leaves

1-2 teaspoons soft brown sugar

You will also need 6 cocktail sticks.

These are delicious served with buttered home-made wholemeal bread and something salady, but they do need to be made a couple of days in advance so that they can marinate and absorb all the flavours.

First of all make the marinade in a saucepan by combining the vinegar, spices, chilli, bay leaves and sugar with 5 fl oz (150 ml) water. Bring to boiling point, then simmer very gently for 5 minutes. Remove from the heat and leave until cold.

Next, sprinkle the herrings with the salt and let them drain in a colander for about 3 hours. After that, rinse off the salt and dry off any excess moisture with kitchen paper. Now cut each dill pickle in three lengthways, spread the filleted side of each fish thinly with mustard and place a piece of dill gherkin and some slices of onion horizontally at what was the head end of each fillet. Then roll up the fillets from the head to the tail end – the skin being on the outside – and secure each roll with a cocktail stick. Pack them into an oval casserole or dish and sprinkle the remaining onion on top. Pour over the marinade, cover the dish, and put it in the lowest part of the fridge. The herrings will not be ready for serving for at least 48 hours and, in fact, they will keep well for at least a week.

Smoked Fish

Smoked Haddock with Crème Fraîche, Chive and Butter Sauce
Serves 2

12-14 oz (350-400 g) undyed smoked haddock or smoked cod, skinned, or same weight golden haddock cutlets, skinned

2 rounded tablespoons crème fraîche

1 heaped tablespoon snipped fresh chives

½ oz (10 g) butter, diced

5 fl oz (150 ml) whole milk

freshly milled black pepper

This is a great recipe, firstly, because it's the most wonderful combination of flavours, and secondly, because it takes only 12 minutes from start to finish. Serve it with spinach cooked in its own juices with a little butter, then drained well, and you'll have a sublime meal in no time at all.

First, place the fish in a large frying pan (10 inches/25.5 cm) and add a little black pepper but no salt. Then pour in the milk (it won't cover the fish, but that doesn't matter), bring it up to simmering point and simmer gently, uncovered, for 8-12 minutes if you're using pieces of smoked haddock or cod, or 8 minutes for golden haddock cutlets. You will be able to see quite clearly when they are cooked, as the whole thing will become pale and opaque.

Now carefully remove the fish to a plate, using a fish slice, increase the heat and add the crème fraîche to the pan. Continue to simmer, uncovered, for 2-3 minutes, until the sauce reduces and thickens slightly, then whisk in the butter and return the fish to the sauce briefly. Scatter in the chives, let it bubble for about 30 seconds and it's ready to serve.

Luxury Smoked Fish Pie
Serves 6

8 oz (225 g) undyed smoked haddock fillet

2 kipper fillets

8 oz (225 g) Arbroath smokies

8 oz (225 g) smoked salmon

15 fl oz (425 ml) whole milk

1 bay leaf

6 black peppercorns

a few stalks of fresh parsley

2 eggs, hard-boiled and chopped

1 heaped tablespoon salted capers, rinsed and patted dry

4 cornichons, drained and chopped

1 tablespoon lemon juice

a few sprigs of fresh watercress, to garnish

salt and freshly milled black pepper

For the sauce

2 oz (50 g) butter

2 oz (50 g) plain flour

5 fl oz (150 ml) single cream

3 tablespoons chopped fresh parsley

For the topping

2 lb (900 g) Desirée potatoes,

2 oz (50 g) butter

2 tablespoons crème fraîche

1 oz (25 g) Gruyère, finely grated

1 tablespoon finely grated Parmesan

You will also need a baking dish, 9 inches (23 cm) square and 2 inches (5 cm) deep, buttered.

Pre-heat the oven to gas mark 6, 400°F (200°C).

I first introduced this in 1978, but I've changed it into less of a family supper dish and into something more suitable for entertaining. Serve it with fresh, shelled peas.

First of all, arrange the haddock in a baking tin, pour over the milk and add the bay leaf, peppercorns and parsley stalks, then bake, uncovered, on a high shelf of the oven for 10 minutes. Meanwhile, remove the skin from the kipper fillets and skin and bone the Arbroath smokies – the flesh will come off very easily. Then chop them into 2 inch (5 cm) pieces, along with the smoked salmon, if the slices are whole, then place all the prepared fish in a mixing bowl. Next, when the haddock is cooked, strain off the liquid and reserve it, discarding the bay leaf, parsley stalks and peppercorns. Then, when the haddock is cool enough to handle, remove the skin and flake the flesh into largish pieces, adding it to the bowl to join the rest of the fish.

Next, make the sauce. Do this by melting the butter in the saucepan, stir in the flour and gradually add the fish liquid bit by bit, stirring continuously. When all the liquid is in, finish the sauce by gradually adding the single cream, then some seasoning, and simmer for 3-4 minutes, then stir in the chopped parsley. Now add the hard-boiled eggs, capers and cornichons to the fish, followed by the lemon juice and, finally, the sauce. Mix it all together gently and carefully so as not to break up the fish too much, then taste and check the seasoning and pour the mixture into the baking dish.

Now, to make the topping, peel and quarter the potatoes, put in a steamer fitted over a large saucepan of boiling water, sprinkle with a dessertspoon of salt, put a lid on and steam until they are absolutely tender – about 25 minutes. Then remove the potatoes from the steamer, drain off the water, return them to the saucepan and cover with a clean tea cloth to absorb some of the steam for about 5 minutes. Now add the butter and crème fraîche and, on the lowest speed, use an electric hand whisk to break the potatoes up, then increase the speed to high and whip them up to a smooth, creamy, fluffy mass. Taste, season well, then spread the potatoes all over the fish, making a ridged pattern with a palette knife. Now finally sprinkle over the grated cheeses and bake on a high shelf in the oven for 30-40 minutes, or until the top is nicely tinged brown. Serve each portion garnished with the watercress.

Kipper Fish Cakes
Serves 4

1 lb (450 g) kipper fillets

1 lb (450 g) Desirée or
King Edward potatoes

1 large egg, hard-boiled and
chopped

2 teaspoons made-up English
mustard

2 teaspoons grated onion

1 tablespoon salted capers or
capers in vinegar, rinsed, patted
dry and chopped

2 tablespoons chopped
fresh parsley

1-2 tablespoons double cream

cayenne pepper

little grated nutmeg

about 2 tablespoons groundnut
or other flavourless oil

about ½ oz (10 g) butter

salt

To garnish

a few sprigs of fresh watercress

lemon quarters

Fish cakes are so popular you can't have too many versions, so here's another one, using kippers, which blend perfectly with potatoes and eggs.

First, peel and quarter the potatoes, then put them in a steamer fitted over a large saucepan of boiling water, sprinkle with a dessertspoon of salt, put a lid on and steam until they are absolutely tender – about 25 minutes. Then remove the potatoes from the steamer, drain off the water, return them to the saucepan and cover with a clean tea cloth to absorb some of the steam for about 5 minutes. Now place the potatoes in a bowl with the egg, mustard, onion, capers, parsley and a tablespoon of the cream.

Now remove the skin from the kippers and flake the fish, discarding any bones and add the flesh to the potato mixture. Beat with a fork until everything is well combined, then season to taste with cayenne and nutmeg, adding the other tablespoon of cream if the mixture seems a little dry. Then press the mixture into about 12 small cakes.

Next, in a large frying pan, heat the oil and butter over a high heat and, when it is really hot, add half the fish cakes to the pan, then turn the heat down to medium and give them 4 minutes' shallow frying on each side. Then drain on crumpled greaseproof paper and keep warm. Repeat with the rest of the fish cakes, adding a little more oil and butter, if needed.

To serve, garnish with sprigs of watercress and lemon quarters (for squeezing the juice over the fish cakes) and have more cayenne pepper available for those who like it.

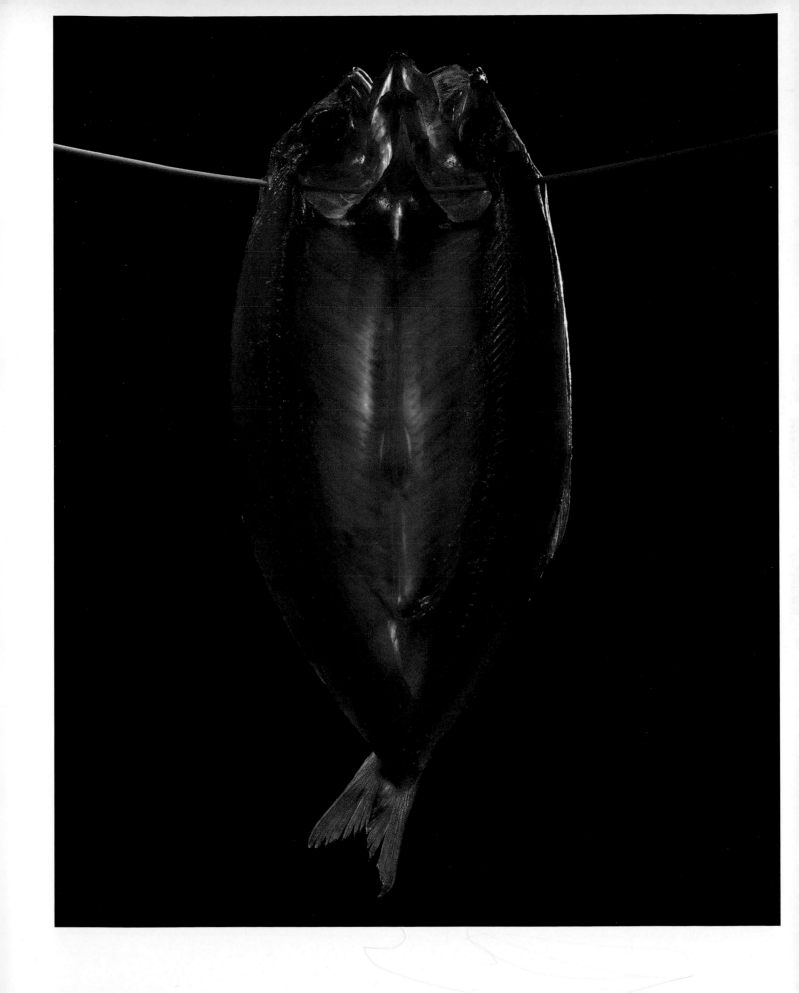

Smoked Fish Tart
with a Parmesan Crust
Serves 4-6 as a main course or 6-8 as a starter

For the pastry

1 oz (25 g) finely grated Parmesan

4 oz (110 g) plain flour, plus a little extra for dusting

a pinch of salt

1 oz (25 g) softened lard

1 oz (25 g) softened butter

For the filling

8 oz (225 g) undyed smoked haddock, skinned

4 oz (110 g) kipper fillet, skinned

9 oz (250 g) smoked salmon trimmings

2 fl oz (55 ml) milk

1 bay leaf

a pinch of ground mace

2 large eggs, plus 2 egg yolks, lightly beaten together

a little ground nutmeg

7 fl oz (200 ml) crème fraîche or double cream

1 dessertspoon salted capers or capers in vinegar, rinsed and patted dry

2 cornichons, drained and finely chopped

freshly milled black pepper

You will also need a 7½ inch (19 cm) diameter, fluted quiche tin with a removable base, 1¼ inches (3 cm) deep, very lightly buttered, and a small, solid baking sheet.

The various smoked flavours of the fish in this tart are quite sensational partnered with the hint of piquancy in the cornichons and capers.

First of all, make the pastry. Sift the flour with the pinch of salt into a large bowl, holding the sieve up high to give it a good airing. Then add the lard and butter and, using only your fingertips, lightly and gently rub the fat into the flour, again lifting the mixture up high all the time to give it a good airing. When everything is crumbly, add the Parmesan and then sprinkle in some cold water – about 1 tablespoon. Start to mix the pastry with a knife and then finish off with your hands, adding more drops of water till you have a smooth dough that will leave the bowl clean. Then pop the pastry into a polythene bag and let it rest in the fridge for 30 minutes.

Meanwhile, pre-heat the oven to gas mark 5, 375°F (190°C) and pop the baking sheet in to pre-heat on the centre shelf.

After that, roll the pastry out into a circle on a surface lightly dusted with flour and, as you roll, give it quarter turns to keep the round shape, rolling it as thinly as possible. Now transfer it, rolling it over the pin, to the tin. Press it lightly and firmly all over the base and sides of the tin, easing any overlapping pastry back down to the sides, as it is important not to stretch it too much. Now trim the edges and press the pastry up about ¼ inch (5 mm) above the rim of the tin all round. Then prick the base all over with a fork and, after that, brush some of the beaten egg for the filling all over the base and sides. Now place the tin on the baking sheet and bake it for 20-25 minutes or until the pastry is crisp and golden. Check halfway through the cooking time to make sure that the pastry isn't rising up in the centre. If it is, just prick it again a couple of times and press it back down again with your hands. When the pastry is cooked, remove the tin from the oven and lower the temperature to gas mark 3, 325°F (170°C).

For the filling, put the haddock and kipper in a medium saucepan, along with the milk, bay leaf and mace. Now bring it up to simmering point, cover with a lid and poach gently for about 2 minutes, then remove the fish from the milk. Discard the bay leaf, but reserve the milk. Then lightly mix the eggs and egg yolks with a seasoning of black pepper and nutmeg, but no salt, as the fish will be fairly salty. Then heat the reserved milk, whisking in the crème fraîche or double cream. Then, when it has come to simmering point, pour it over the beaten eggs, whisking well.

Now divide the cooked haddock and kipper into flakes about ½ inch (1 cm) in size and arrange them in the cooked pastry case, along with the smoked salmon trimmings. Next, scatter the capers and cornichons all over and slowly pour half the cream and egg mixture in, allowing the liquid to settle between each addition. Then place the baking sheet in the oven, gradually add the remainder of the filling and cook for 30-35 minutes or until the surface is golden brown and feels firm in the centre.

When you have removed it from the oven, let it rest for 10 minutes, then ease it away from the edges using a small knife, and place the tin on a suitably sized jar, which will allow you to carefully ease the sides away. Then slide a palette knife or wide fish slice underneath and ease the tart carefully on to a plate or board ready to serve, or simply cut it into portions straight from the tin base.

Mixed Smoked Fish Kedgeree with a Crème Fraîche and Parsley Sauce
Serves 4

1 lb (450 g) undyed smoked haddock

4 oz (110 g) kipper fillets

4½ oz (125 g) smoked salmon trimmings

3 large eggs

1 pint (570 ml) milk

1 bay leaf

white basmati rice, measured to the 8 fl oz (225 ml) level in a glass measuring jug

salt and freshly milled black pepper

For the parsley sauce

¾ oz (20 g) butter

¾ oz (20 g) plain flour

10 fl oz (275 ml) milk (reserved from poaching the fish)

7 fl oz (200 ml) crème fraîche

2 tablespoons chopped fresh parsley

The combination of smoked haddock, kippers and smoked salmon makes for a fuller flavoured kedgeree and, because the classic version can sometimes be a bit dry, the addition of the creamy sauce really does make this one very special.

Start off by boiling the eggs: the best way to achieve slightly creamy yolks is to place the eggs in cold water, bring them up to the boil, then boil them for 6 minutes. After that, cool them under cold running water. Next, place the milk in a saucepan with the bay leaf and some black pepper (don't put any salt in it as the fish is already quite salty), add the haddock and poach it for 2-3 minutes after it comes up to simmering point. Then add the kipper fillets and smoked salmon and simmer for a further minute. Now remove the bay leaf and then drain off the poaching milk – use the lid on the saucepan to enable you to strain it off through a small gap into a measuring jug. Then remove the skin from the fish and divide the flesh into largish chunks. Place these in a dish, together with the peeled and halved or quartered eggs, cover with foil and keep everything warm in a low oven or a warming drawer. It's a good idea to pop the serving dishes in to warm as well at this stage.

Next, place the rice in a shallow pan with a lid. Reserve 10 fl oz (275 ml) of the poaching milk for the sauce, then make the rest up to 16 fl oz (450 ml) with boiling water. Pour this on to the rice, add some salt, bring it up to simmering point and cook for 15 minutes exactly with the lid on.

While that is happening, make the sauce by melting the butter in a small saucepan, then stir in the flour with a wooden spoon till you have a smooth paste. After that, add the reserved milk, a little at a time, still stirring, until you have a smooth, thickened sauce. Let it cook very gently for 2 minutes before stirring in the crème fraîche and parsley, then taste to check the seasoning.

Now it's an assembly job. First, place the cooked rice in a serving dish, followed by the smoked fish and eggs and finally pour some of the sauce over – take the rest in a jug to the table to allow people to help themselves.

Highland Pasta with Smoked Salmon

Serves 2 as a main course or 4 as a starter

4 oz (110 g) dried pasta (such as macaroni, penne or rigatoni)

8 oz (225 g) smoked salmon

1 oz (25 g) butter

1 medium onion, finely chopped

1 clove garlic, crushed with 1 teaspoon salt

4 oz (110 g) chestnut mushrooms, thinly sliced

1 teaspoon mild curry powder

1 tablespoon plain flour

5 fl oz (150 ml) dry white wine

2 tablespoons crème fraîche

salt

I was given this recipe when I went to the Isle of Skye to write about salmon farming on the Strathaird Estate. It makes a very special and extremely quick supper dish for two people, or it can be served as a starter for four.

Begin by melting the butter in a solid-based frying pan, then add the onion and sauté over a low heat until soft. This will take about 7 minutes. Now add the crushed garlic and mushrooms and continue to cook for a further 2-3 minutes. Next, mix the curry powder and flour together and stir these into the butter to soak up all the juices. Then add the wine gradually, stirring briskly after each addition and, when all the wine is added, cook for a further 3 minutes before finally adding the crème fraîche. The sauce is now ready and can be made up to this stage in advance, but lay a piece of clingfilm over the surface if you're not using it immediately.

When you're ready to cook the pasta, place a large saucepan with plenty of lightly salted water on to boil and cook the pasta for 10-12 minutes or until it is cooked to your liking, but still retains some bite. Meanwhile, tear little pieces of smoked salmon lengthways into strips, then re-heat the sauce and add the salmon at the very last minute, just before serving. Now, drain the pasta, return it to the pan, then quickly stir in the sauce and smoked salmon and serve at once in deep, heated bowls.

Marinated Kipper Fillets and Potato Salad with Coriander Seeds and Cracked Pepper

Serves 4 as a main course or 8 as a starter

6 kipper fillets

2 teaspoons coriander seeds

2 teaspoons black peppercorns

6 shallots or 1 medium onion, cut into thin rings

2 bay leaves, each snipped into 3-4 pieces

1 lemon, thinly sliced

a few sprigs of fresh thyme and flat-leaf parsley

juice of 2 lemons

1 dessertspoon dark soft brown sugar

2 rounded teaspoons wholegrain mustard

5 fl oz (150 ml) extra virgin olive oil

To serve

1 lb 8 oz (700 g) new potatoes, scrubbed but skins left on

a few sprigs of fresh flat-leaf parsley

sea salt

You will also need a shallow dish with a capacity of 1½ pints (850 ml).

This is a salad that can mostly be made way, way ahead – up to a week, believe it or not. Then all you do is steam some potatoes to go with it or, alternatively, you can serve the kipper fillets as they are, and instead of the potatoes, have a pile of buttered wholemeal bread on the table.

To get the best fragrance from the coriander seeds and peppercorns, pop them in a small frying pan and place them over a medium heat to dry-roast for 2-3 minutes. Move them around the pan until they start to jump, then put them in a pestle and mortar and crush them fairly coarsely.

Next, prepare the kipper fillets by turning them skin side up on a flat surface, then, with a sharp knife, lift the skin away at the tail end. Now, discard the knife and simply pull the skin from the flesh. If it clings at any point, just use the knife again and ease it away. Now snip each one in 4 lengthways, then cut them into 1½ inch (4 cm) pieces and lay the strips in the dish – this will probably have to be in 2 layers to fit them in – sprinkling the pepper and coriander mixture all over each layer. Next, scatter the shallot or onion rings, bay leaves, lemon slices, sprigs of thyme and parsley all over, tucking them in between the kipper fillets here and there. Now, in a bowl, whisk together the lemon juice, sugar, mustard and oil and, when they're very thoroughly mixed, pour the mixture over the kippers. Cover with clingfilm and put a plate on top with some kind of weight on it to keep the kippers submerged, then place in the fridge and let them marinate for a minimum of 24 hours or up to a week.

When you want to serve the salad, it's important to remove the kippers from the fridge at least an hour beforehand. Now steam the potatoes, generously sprinkled with sea salt, for 20-30 minutes (depending on their size) and, when they're cooked, place a clean tea cloth over them to absorb the steam for 5 minutes. Chop them roughly, divide them among the plates, spoon some of the kipper marinade over, then arrange the kippers and everything else on top. Finish off with a few sprigs of flat-leaf parsley.

Simon Hopkinson's Smoked Haddock with Spinach
Serves 4

4 pieces undyed smoked haddock (about 6 oz/175 g each), skinned and boned

10 fl oz (275 ml) milk

freshly milled black pepper

For the sauce

2 tablespoons chopped fresh chives

6 oz (175 g) butter

3 large egg yolks

1 tablespoon lemon juice

salt and freshly milled black pepper

For the spinach

2 lb (900 g) spinach, picked over, trimmed and thoroughly washed

1 oz (25 g) butter

salt and freshly milled black pepper

My thanks to cookery writer and dear friend Simon Hopkinson for this superb recipe, which he cooked for me at Bibendum one day for lunch – and had invented that day! Due to his generosity, all of us can make and savour what has become one of my very favourite fish recipes.

First, you need to make the sauce: place the butter in a small saucepan and let it melt slowly. Meanwhile, blend the egg yolks and seasoning in a blender or food processor.

Now turn the heat up and when the butter reaches the boil, pour it into a jug and start to pour this very slowly into the blender, in a thin trickle, with the motor running, until all the butter is added and the sauce is thickened. Next, with the motor still switched on, slowly add the lemon juice. Then keep the sauce warm by placing it in a basin over some hot water.

To cook the fish, place it in a frying pan, pour in the milk, add some freshly milled pepper, then bring it all up to a gentle simmer. Cover and poach for 6-7 minutes. While that is happening, cook the spinach – melt the butter in a large saucepan and pile the spinach in with a teaspoon of salt and some freshly milled black pepper. Put the lid on and cook it over a medium heat for 2-3 minutes, turning it all over half way through. Quite a bit of water will come out, so what you need to do then is drain it in a colander and press down a small plate on top to squeeze out every last bit of juice. Cover with a clean tea cloth and keep warm.

When the haddock is ready, divide the spinach among 4 warm serving plates, and place the haddock pieces on top. Now just add a little of the poaching liquid (about 2 tablespoons) to the sauce and whisk it in along with the chives, then pour the sauce over the haddock and spinach. Serve straightaway.

Note This recipe contains raw eggs.

Smoked Salmon Tart

Serves 4 as a main course or 6 as a starter

For the Parmesan pastry

1 oz (25 g) Parmesan, finely grated

4 oz (110 g) plain flour

a pinch of salt

1 oz (25 g) softened lard

1 oz (25 g) softened butter

For the filling

9 oz (250 g) smoked salmon trimmings

2 large eggs, plus 1 extra yolk, lightly beaten together

7 fl oz (200 ml) crème fraîche

freshly grated nutmeg

a pinch of cayenne pepper

freshly milled black pepper

You will also need a 9½ inch (24 cm), loose-bottomed quiche tin, 1 inch (2 cm) deep, lightly greased, and a solid baking sheet.

Pre-heat the oven to gas mark 5, 375°F (190°C), with the baking sheet on the centre shelf.

The secret of a great tart or quiche is a perfect pastry base – crisp, light and flaky, without a hint of sogginess – to offset the rich, creamy filling. Here is the best of both worlds – a luscious smoked salmon tart that's simplicity itself.

To make the pastry, sift the flour with a pinch of salt into a large bowl, holding the sieve up high to give the flour a good airing. Then add the lard and butter and, using only your fingertips, lightly and gently rub the fat into the flour, again lifting the mixture up high all the time to give it a good airing. When everything is crumbly, add the Parmesan and then sprinkle in some cold water – about 1 tablespoon. Start to mix the pastry with a knife and then finish off with your hands, adding more drops of water till you have a smooth dough that will leave the bowl clean. Then pop it into a polythene bag and let it rest in the fridge for 30 minutes. After that, roll the pastry out into a circle about 12 inches (30 cm) in diameter, then transfer it, rolling it over the pin, to the tin. Press lightly and firmly over the base and sides of the tin, pushing up the sides to come about ¼ inch (5 mm) above the rim of the tin all round. Now prick the base all over with a fork, then brush with some of the beaten egg for the filling. Place the tin on the pre-heated baking sheet and bake it for 20-25 minutes or until the pastry is crisp and golden. Check halfway through the cooking time to make sure the pastry isn't rising in the centre. If it is, just prick it a couple of times and press it back down with your hands.

When the pastry case is cooked, remove it from the oven and reduce the heat to gas mark 4, 350°F (180°C). Now arrange the smoked salmon over the base of the tart. Then, in a jug, mix the eggs with the crème fraîche and season with black pepper and a little freshly grated nutmeg, but no salt, as the smoked salmon is already quite salty. Now pop the tart back on the half-pulled-out oven shelf, then pour in the egg mixture and sprinkle with the cayenne pepper. Bake it for 30-35 minutes until the centre is just set and the surface is puffy and golden, then remove it from the oven and let it settle for about 10 minutes before serving. Remove it from the tin by placing it on an upturned jar, which will allow you to ease the sides away. Using a palette knife or a fish slice, slide it underneath and ease the tart carefully on to a plate or board, ready to serve.

Easy Omelette Arnold Bennett
Serves 2 as a supper dish or 3 as a light lunch

2 rounded tablespoons
crème fraîche

8 oz (225 g) undyed smoked
haddock, skin and bones removed,
cut into ½ inch (1 cm) chunks

5 large eggs

½ teaspoon cornflour

½ oz (10 g) butter

1 teaspoon olive oil

2 oz (50 g) Gruyère, grated

salt and freshly milled
black pepper

You will also need an 8 inch
(20 cm) omelette pan or frying pan.

This is actually a famous classic, created – so the story goes – for the novelist Arnold Bennett, who wrote an entire novel, *Imperial Palace*, while staying at the Savoy hotel. While his work was in progress, the chefs perfected the omelette to such a degree that our friend demanded that it be made for him wherever he travelled anywhere in the world and hence its name. Meanwhile, the Savoy Grill, proud of their achievement, still serve it every single day, year in, year out. It is a truly wonderful creation, a flat but fluffy, open-faced omelette made with smoked Finnan haddock. What I have discovered is that, while chefs can instantly call upon a ladle of béchamel or hollandaise (both included in the Savoy recipe), it's quite a fiddle to make all this at home. So I have adapted it so that it becomes much simpler and speedier, but I promise just as brilliant as the original.

To begin with, measure the crème fraîche into a medium saucepan and bring it up to a gentle simmer. Add some freshly milled black pepper, but don't add salt yet, because the haddock can be quite salty. Then pop in the prepared fish and let it poach gently, uncovered, for about 5 minutes. Meanwhile, make up the sauce: separate one of the eggs, breaking the yolk into a small bowl and reserving the white in another bowl. Add the cornflour to the yolk and whisk well.

When the fish is cooked, use a draining spoon to lift it out into a sieve placed over the saucepan, to allow the liquid to drain back. Press lightly to extract every last drop, then place the sieve containing the fish on a plate. At this point, pre-heat the grill to its highest setting. Now bring the liquid in the pan back up to simmering point, then pour it on to the egg yolk, whisking all the time. Then return the whole mixture to the saucepan and gently bring it back to just below simmering point or until it has thickened – no more than 1 or 2 minutes. After that, remove it from the heat and stir in the fish, tasting to see if it needs any salt. Next, whisk up the egg white to the soft-peak stage and carefully fold it in.

Now for the omelette. First, beat the 4 remaining eggs with some seasoning. Next, melt the butter and oil in the frying pan until foaming, swirling them round to coat the sides and base. When it's very hot, add the eggs, let them settle for about 2 minutes, then begin to draw the edges into the centre, tilting the pan to let the liquid egg run into the gaps. When you feel the eggs are half set, turn the heat down and spoon the haddock mixture evenly over the surface of the eggs, using a palette knife to spread it. Now sprinkle the Gruyère over the top and place the pan under the grill, positioning it roughly 5 inches (13 cm) from the heat source. The omelette will now take 2-3 minutes to become puffy, golden brown and bubbling. Remove it from the grill, let it relax for 5 minutes before cutting into wedges and serving it on warmed plates.

Fish Extras

How to bone a whole fish

This method applies to herring, mackerel and trout – it really is dead simple. First, ask the fishmonger to scale and trim the fish.

All you do is cut along the belly of the fish with scissors, snipping off the head, fins and, if you need to, the tail, then place it, flesh side down, on a flat surface.

Now, using a rolling pin, give the fish a few sharp taps to flatten it out. Next, press very firmly with your thumbs or the handle of a wooden spoon **(opposite, top left)** all along the backbone of the fish, which will loosen it.

Now turn the fish skin side down and, using a sharp knife and starting at the head end, gently ease the backbone away **(top right)**, as it comes away, almost all the little bones will come away with it. Any that don't can be removed afterwards, and tweezers are helpful here.

Finally, cut away the dark belly flaps, using scissors **(bottom left)**.

How to skin a fillet of fish

All you need is a flat surface and a sharp knife. First of all, angle the knife at the thinner or tail end of the fillet, or, if it's all the same thickness, just start at one end. Cut a little bit of the flesh away from the skin - enough to get the knife angled in **(opposite, bottom right)**.

Now, using your fingertips, hang on to the skin, clasping it as firmly as possible, then push the knife with your other hand, keeping the blade at an angle. Push at the skin, not the flesh, remembering the skin is tough and the knife won't go through it. What's happening is the knife blade, as it slides between the skin and the flesh, is cutting the skin away.

If you're not experienced, don't worry if you're left with a few patches of skin, you can just gently cut these away. Practice is all you need and you'll soon be able to feel when the angle of the knife is right.

Hollandaise Sauce
Serves 4

This is supremely wonderful with any kind of grilled or poached fish.

2 large egg yolks
1 dessertspoon lemon juice
1 dessertspoon white wine vinegar
4 oz (110 g) butter
salt and freshly milled black pepper

Begin by placing the egg yolks in a food processor or blender and season them with a pinch of salt and pepper (opposite, top left). Then blend them thoroughly for about 1 minute. After that, heat the lemon juice and white wine vinegar in a small saucepan until the mixture starts to bubble and simmer (top right). Switch the processor or blender on again and pour the hot liquid on to the egg yolks in a slow, steady stream. After that, switch the processor or blender off.

Now, using the same saucepan, melt the butter over a gentle heat, being very careful not to let it brown. When the butter is foaming, switch the processor or blender on once more and pour in the butter in a thin, slow, steady trickle; the slower you add it the better (bottom left). If it helps you to use a jug and not pour from the saucepan, warm a jug with boiling water, discard the boiling water and then pour the butter mixture into that first. When all the butter has been incorporated, wipe around the sides of the processor bowl or blender with a spatula to incorporate all the sauce, then give the sauce one more quick burst and you should end up with a lovely, smooth, thick, buttery sauce (bottom right).

Note This recipe contains raw eggs.

Foaming Hollandaise

What happens here is that the egg whites are whisked to soft peaks and folded into the sauce as soon as it's made. The advantages are legion: firstly, it lightens the sauce, so there are not quite so many calories, and you get a greater volume, so it goes further. It will never curdle because the egg whites stabilise the whole thing, which means you can happily keep it warm in a bowl fitted over simmering water. That's not all: you can also re-heat it in the same way and it will even freeze.

Very Quick Home-made Tartare Sauce

Serves 2

This will keep in a clean screw-top jar in the fridge for up to a week.

1 large egg

½ teaspoon sea salt

1 small clove garlic, peeled

½ teaspoon dry mustard powder

6 fl oz (175 ml) light olive oil

1 dessertspoon lemon juice

1 tablespoon fresh flat-leaf parsley leaves

1 heaped tablespoon salted capers, rinsed and patted dry

4 cornichons, drained

freshly milled black pepper

Begin by breaking the egg into a processor or blender, add the salt, garlic and mustard powder, then switch the motor on and, through the feeder tube, add the oil in a thin, steady trickle, pouring it as slowly as you can (it takes about 2 minutes). When the oil is in and the sauce has thickened, add some pepper and all the other ingredients. Now pulse until the ingredients are chopped – as coarsely or as finely as you want. Lastly, taste to check the seasoning, then transfer to a serving bowl.

Coriander and Lime Tartare Sauce

For a quick coriander and lime tartare sauce, replace the lemon juice and parsley with lime juice and fresh coriander. This is lovely used in Californian Grilled Fish (see page 34).

Mexican Tomato Salsa

Serves 4

This is lovely served with plain grilled fish.

4 large, firm tomatoes, skinned and deseeded

1 fresh green chilli, halved and deseeded

½ medium red onion, finely chopped

2 heaped tablespoons chopped fresh coriander

juice of 1 lime

salt and freshly milled black pepper

First, using a sharp knife, chop the tomatoes into approximately ¼ inch (5 mm) dice.

Next, chop the chilli very finely before adding it to the tomatoes. Add the onion, coriander and lime juice, and season with salt and freshly milled black pepper. Give everything a thorough mixing, then cover and leave on one side for about an hour before serving.

Mustard sauce
Serves 4-6

This is a good sauce to serve with oily fish and is particularly excellent as an accompaniment to herrings.

10 fl oz (275 ml) milk

1 small onion, halved

1½ oz (40 g) butter

1 oz (25 g) plain flour

2 rounded teaspoons dry mustard powder

5 fl oz (150 ml) fish or vegetable stock

1 teaspoon lemon juice

salt and cayenne pepper

First of all, pour the milk into a small saucepan and add the halved onion. Then place over a low heat and let it come very slowly up to simmering point, which will take approximately 5 minutes. Then remove the saucepan from the heat and leave the milk to infuse until cooled before straining, discarding the onion.

Now place the milk, together with the butter, flour, mustard powder and stock, into the same washed pan, and bring to the boil whisking continuously. Then cook the sauce gently for 5 minutes. Taste and season with the lemon juice, salt and cayenne.

Tomato and Pesto Sauce
Serves 4

Serve with with grilled, fried or baked fish.

1 lb (450 g) skinned, chopped tomatoes

4 oz (110 g) fresh pesto sauce

salt and freshly milled black pepper

All you do is place the tomatoes in a saucepan with some seasoning, simmer, uncovered, and reduce until thickened for about 10 minutes. Then stir in the fresh pesto sauce, re-heat gently and serve with grilled, fried or baked fish.

Basic Fish Batter
Makes enough for four 6-7 oz (175-200 g) pieces of fish

I have found this very simple flour and water batter is the best of all for deep-frying.

4 oz (110 g) self-raising flour

½ teaspoon salt

Just sift the flour and salt into a mixing bowl, then gradually add 5 fl oz (150 ml) water, plus 1 scant tablespoon, whisking continuously until the batter is smooth and free from lumps.

Conversions for Australia and New Zealand

Measurements in this book refer to British standard imperial and metric measurements.

The standard UK teaspoon measure is 5 ml, the dessertspoon is 10 ml and the tablespoon measure is 15 ml. In Australia, the standard tablespoon is 20 ml.

UK large eggs weigh 63-73 g.

Converting standard cups to imperial and metric weights

Ingredients (1 cup)	Imperial/metric
basil, fresh*	2 oz/50 g
black beans, dried	8 oz /225 g
breadcrumbs, fresh	3 oz/75 g
butter	9 oz/250 g
carrots, finely chopped	5 oz/150 g
celery, sliced	4½ oz/125 g
Cheddar, grated*	4½ oz/125 g
coconut, creamed	9 oz/250 g
coconut milk powder	4 oz/110 g
coriander, chopped	2 oz/50 g
coriander, fresh, leaves	1 oz/25 g
couscous	6½ oz/185 g
flour	4½ oz/125 g
grapes	6 oz/175 g
Gruyère, grated	4½ oz/125 g
hazelnuts, whole	4¾ oz/140 g
lard	9 oz/250 g
leeks, sliced	4 oz /110 g
lentils, Puy	7 oz/200 g
mushrooms, small, sliced	3½ oz/95 g
oatmeal	4½ oz/125 g
olives, pitted	4½ oz/125 g
onion, chopped	5 oz/150 g
parsley, flat leaf, whole	¾ oz/20 g
Parmesan, finely grated	4 oz/110 g
polenta	5 oz/150 g
peas, fresh, shelled	5 oz /150 g
rice, raw, long grain	7 oz/200 g
rocket leaves*	1½ oz/40 g
sorrel leaves*	2 oz/50 g
spinach, raw, baby English*	2 oz/50 g
tomatoes, fresh, chopped	7 oz/200 g
tomatoes, sun-dried, whole	5 oz/150 g
tomatoes, tinned, chopped	9 oz/250 g

*Firmly packed

Liquid cup conversions

Metric	Imperial	Cups
30 ml	1 fl oz	⅛ cup
60 ml	2 fl oz	¼ cup
80 ml	2¾ fl oz	⅓ cup
125 ml	4 fl oz	½ cup
185 ml	6 fl oz	¾ cup
250 ml	8 fl oz	1 cup
375 ml	12 fl oz	1½ cups
315 ml	10 fl oz	1¼ cups
500 ml	16 fl oz	2 cups
600 ml	1 pint	2½ cups
750 ml	24 fl oz	3 cups
1 litre	32 fl oz	4 cups

A few ingredient names

Arbroath smokies
use extra kipper fillet

cod
use Blue cod

Desirée potatoes
use other waxy, fleshed potatoes

double/whipping cream
use thick cream

haddock
use Blue cod or hoki

halibut
use salmon or grouper

pepper, red/yellow/green
capsicum

plaice or sole
use flounder

salmon
Atlantic salmon

sea bass
use snapper, hapuku or jewfish

single cream
use thin cream

smoked haddock
use smoked cod

spring onions
salad onion/shallots

tiger prawns
use other medium prawns

whiting
use flathead or Blue Whiting

Index

Miki Duisterhof   6, 14, 28, 32, 36, 39,
40, 44, 49, 63, 68, 70, 74, 78, 82, 89,
94, 98, 102, 107, 117, 124, 128
Tony Heathcote   117
Peter Knab   6, 9, 13, 17, 18, 20/21, 23,
24, 28, 40, 43, 54, 57, 59, 64, 67, 70,
73, 81, 84/85, 90, 98, 101, 108/109,
110, 114, 118, 122/123, 127, 128, 130
Jonathan Lovekin   6, 23
Jason Lowe   40
J P Masclet   137
S & O Matthews   6, 110
David Munns   70, 98
Michael Paul   6, 10, 13, 28, 31, 35, 40,
47, 53, 59, 60, 70, 77, 78, 86, 93, 97,
98, 113, 117, 128, 133
Simon Smith   27
Dan Stevens   70
Patrice de Villiers   105
Cameron Watt   6, 13, 50, 121
Rob White   70, 98

Delia Smith is Britain's best-selling cookery author, whose books have sold over 16 million copies. Delia's other books include *How To Cook Books One*, *Two* and *Three*, her *Vegetarian Collection*, the *Complete Illustrated Cookery Course*, *One Is Fun*, the *Summer* and *Winter Collections* and *Christmas*. She has launched her own website. She is also a director of Norwich City Football Club, where she is in charge of Canary Catering, several restaurants and a regular series of food and wine workshops.

She is married to the writer and editor Michael Wynn Jones and they live in Suffolk.

For more information on Delia's restaurant,
food and wine workshops and events, contact:
Delia's Canary Catering, Norwich City Football Club, Carrow Road,
Norwich NR1 1JE; www.deliascanarycatering.co.uk
For Delia's Canary Catering (conferencing and events enquiries),
telephone 01603 218704
For Delia's Restaurant and Bar (reservations),
telephone 01603 218705

Visit Delia's website at www.deliaonline.com